Present in His Presence

Devotional

Lisa Buffaloe

Present in His Presence

Copyright 2017 Lisa Buffaloe (updated July 2023)
John 15:11 Publications, Florence, AL 35630

All rights reserved. No part of this book may be reproduced or transmitted in any way, form or by any means, electronic or mechanical—including photocopying, recording, or by any information storage and retrieval system— except brief quotations in printed reviews. without permission of the author.

Visit the author's website at https://lisabuffaloe.com

Cover photo: Lisa Buffaloe
Cover design: Scott Buffaloe

ISBN-13: 978-0692995990
ISBN-10: 0692995994

Printed in the United States of America

To our wonderful Heavenly Father. Thank You for inviting us into Your presence through the gift of grace through Your Son, Jesus Christ.

"My heart has heard you say, 'Come and talk with me.' And my heart responds, 'Lord, I am coming.'"
~ Psalm 27:8 (NLT)

Contents

Welcome 1
Unwrap the present.. 2
Battles will rage 5
Don't grow weary 8
Owed and offended.. 11
Love them to Life 15
But God... 17
Storm comfort 19
Waving... 22
Profitable... 24
What's in your hand?... 26
Don't get under the wrong wing! 29
Humble prayers 30
It will make a difference 32
If you only knew.. 34
True knowledge 36
Resonate.. 38
Happy dancing from the rooftops 41
Staying silent.. 43
Finding Hope 46
Small beginnings.. 49
Knowing isn't enough 51
You are loved.. 53
I'm always here... 55
Worth it 58
It's not what you think 60
Soul-rehydration 63
I don't understand 66
Known 68
Heart attack 70
Following 72

What was done	74
Fight the good fight	76
Grudge nursing	80
Reflectors	82
Casting	84
The worst thing	86
Light us up!	88
Fast-food	91
Flooding Fear	93
Cut the chains	97
My time	99
Withheld to be held	101
Never dry	104
Not	108
The old	111
Celebrating holidays	115
Loving All	118
Recalculating	121
Come to the Manger	124
Dance of the frail	127
Thank you	129
About the Author	130
Books by Lisa Buffaloe	131
Bible credits	132

Welcome

Thank you for your interest in reading this book. I know your time is valuable. I'm honored you're here. I've written this devotional to hopefully help you find the presents of God's presence gifted each day.

After each devotion are blessings from God's Word (His Present), along with additional thoughts, quotes, or questions to unwrap His truths for further study.

My words are mere words, yet God's truth, the Word, is living water and bread of life to feed your soul. Read and linger slow in the gifts God gives through His Word and His truth, for Jesus promises the truth will set you free.

My prayer as you read, that God's truth will set you free to enjoy each day given. Be present in the joys of God's presence.

Welcome!

Unwrap the present

Anyone else have a hard time living in the present? Is it just me? Good grief, the past keeps trying to creep into today and future concerns try to keep me wrapped up in the worries of tomorrow. The past and future squeezes me out of today which keeps me from living in the day. Ugh.

I really want to be fully present in the present. I've tried various ways, tried to give it my all, focus my mind, get rid of distractions, but the only thing that works, the only way I've found success is by seeking God's presence. Thankfully, it's not an art that needs to be mastered on our own, God's presence is fully present. If I seek God, calm my soul in Him, then I am wrapped in His presence in the present.

We can't physically live in the past or the future, our bodies are here in the now, today, and we have a choice where we focus and how we live. God heals the past – our mistakes, our sins, the sins others have committed against us. God knows the future, is already in the future, and will help us through whatever comes in the future. As we embrace the light of His presence, all things are lit by His presence.

Today is a gift, it is the present. Unwrap today, the present, by being in the presence of God.

"My heart has heard you say, 'Come and talk with me.' And my heart responds, 'Lord, I am coming.'" ~ Psalm 27:8 (NLT)

His Present

God is the great I AM. He is and was and is to come. He is eternally present. Seek God and you will find Him. Rest in God (even in your restless moments) and you will find His rest. His joy, His presence, all are gifts for you.

God blesses with the beauty of His creation as an example of His loving care. Read what Jesus shares in the following passage. How can these truths help you fully embrace today?

Jesus said, "If God gives such attention to the appearance of wildflowers—most of which are never even seen—don't you think he'll attend to you, take pride in you, do his best for you? What I'm trying to do here is to get you to relax, to not be so preoccupied .... People who don't know God and the way he works fuss over these things, but you know both God and how he works. Steep your life in God-reality, God initiative, God-provisions. ... You'll find all your everyday human concerns will be met. Give your entire attention to what God is doing right now, and don't get worked up about what may or may not happen tomorrow. God will help you deal with whatever hard things come up when the time comes. ~ Matthew 6:32-34 (MSG)

What does the Psalmist share about God's presence? "You will show me the path of life; in Your presence is fullness of joy; at Your right hand are pleasures forevermore." ~ Psalm 16:11 (NKJV)

God's word promises, the closer we draw to God, the more we seek His presence, the more we find a deep, intimate, vibrant, free-flowing, loving relationship and friendship. The present is now, and God is here, the Great I AM is here now, waiting for you.

"Sing praises to God and to his name! Sing loud praises to him who rides the clouds. His name is the LORD— rejoice in his presence!" ~ Psalm 68:4 (NLT)

Battles will rage

Battles, battles, everywhere are battles. Yikes, ack, whimper. The world seems to have gone stark raving mad.

I have good news, the battles will rage, but the final war has been won. Victory has been declared, victory has been won, for the ending has been given by God and no one can change what God has declared. Evil will be punished, and the righteous will come Home to eternal paradise.

We are not called to fight every battle; we are strategically placed throughout the globe to be strategically used by God to tell the Good News that Jesus saves. We are placed here and now in the world to tell the world there is One who offers grace, mercy, forgiveness and saves the world.

Although Satan uses people to accomplish his devious plans, we do not fight with flesh and blood. We can battle in the heavenlies, and the power of heaven is always, always, ***always*** greater in us than the enemy. God is greater, God is victorious, and we fight from God's victory.

Our power, our might isn't what is needed, we don't have to be super-people, we only need to rest in the power of our All-Mighty God.

Battles rage all around us, it's hard to stand, so difficult to fight, but please remember you are never alone, you are never without hope, and God is mighty to save. If you are in a battle, trust that God will bring you through that battle, and every battle, to victory.

His Present

Paul reminds us of our victory in Christ -- victory that covers us with God's love in every area of our lives. As you ponder the following passage, consider the battles you currently face. Plug in the truths from God word and pray them back to God. In prayer and praise, the truth will set you free.

Remember, "we have complete victory through him who loved us! For I am convinced that neither death, nor life, nor angels, nor heavenly rulers, nor things that are present, nor things to come, nor powers, nor height, nor depth, nor anything else in creation will be able to separate us from the love of God in Christ Jesus our Lord." ~ Romans 8:37-39 (NET Bible)

As a Christian, you are a victor and conqueror. Victory is something that comes after a battle, conqueror is what you are in battle.

Whatever battle you are in, or are facing, remember you are a victorious conqueror in the power of Christ. In what ways does this give you a new perspective?

"Thanks be to God, who gives us the victory [making us conquerors] through our Lord Jesus Christ." ~ 1 Corinthians 15:57 (AMPC)

God is not only your protector, He also trains you and prepares you for the battles you face. You are loved and sheltered in the strong refuge of God's deliverance.

"The Lord, my protector, deserves praise—the one who trains my hands for battle, and my fingers for war, who loves me and is my stronghold, my refuge and my deliverer, my shield and the one in whom I take shelter..." ~ Psalm 144:1-2 (NET Bible)

Don't grow weary

The Bible encourages us not to grow weary. "Let us not lose heart in doing good, for in due time we will reap if we do not grow weary ... do not grow weary of doing good. ... For consider Him who has endured such hostility by sinners against Himself, so that you will not grow weary and lose heart." ~ Galatians 6:9, 2 Thessalonians 3:13, Hebrews 12:3

I wondered; how do you not grow weary? Some days it seems hard to even breathe. Then I realized, I need to keep my focus on Jesus who kept going until He fulfilled His purpose.

While I am here on this earth, no matter how I feel, I can keep weary thoughts from growing. I don't need to plant weary, don't need to tend weary, and sure don't want weary to grow. By staying in God's Word, anchored deep in His truth, I remember God is greater than any enemy and any difficulty, God's love never fails, and He is in control.

God's power is inexhaustible and as a Christian, we have God's power through the power of Christ. When our bodies and spirits are weary, cast down, and barely hanging on, hope in God. God's hope is unfailing.

God loves you. He won't leave you or forsake you. Hang onto God, and even when you can't hang on, He will never let you fall. You are always safe in His loving, always faithful, always true, always grace-filled, nail-scarred hands.

Bodies may grow weary, but our spirits are infused with unlimited, infinite, endless, amazing power of God. Fly in the truth of God's power and might.

His Present

God's word doesn't deny the fact your body grows tired and weary, however the beauty of those who trust and wait on God will find His strength. Read the verse below and insert your name, make the promise personal for you.

Even "though youths grow weary and tired, and vigorous young men stumble badly, yet those who wait for the Lord will gain new strength; they will mount up with wings like eagles, they will run and not get tired, they will walk and not become weary." ~ Isaiah 40:30-31 (NASB)

Where does the Psalmist find hope in Psalm 42:11?

"Why are you cast down, O my inner self? And why should you moan over me and be disquieted within me? Hope in God and wait expectantly for Him, for I shall yet praise Him, Who is the help of my countenance, and my God." ~ Psalm 42:11 (AMPC)

Based on the verse following in Habakkuk, what are the ways God's strength gives you strength?

"The Lord God is my Strength, my personal bravery, and my invincible army; He makes my feet like hinds' feet and will make me to walk [not to stand still in terror, but to walk] and make [spiritual] progress upon my high places [of trouble, suffering, or responsibility]!" ~ Habakkuk 3:19 (AMPC)

Owed and offended

The devil wants people to believe the world, and God, owes them something, and therefore, they have the right to be offended. Satan wants people to think God is uncaring, insensitive, unaware, distant and is holding out on them. The more the enemy can keep people feeling owed and offended, the more people are provoked. Negativity and offenses spread like wildfire by the pit of hell to send as many as possible to the pit of hell.

The enemy spends his time wreaking havoc in the world, abusing, terrorizing, putting out negative news about the terrible things the devil does, then pointing to God that it's all His fault.

If you are a Christian, you are safe from hell, but the enemy can make you think you live in hell on earth if you don't keep a heavenly perspective. Anything that causes you to feel owed and offended, did **not** come from God.

If you are going to think about anything, share anything, ponder anything, let it be God's truth. Stand on the solid foundation of God's truth. God's Word is truth, and His truth sets you free.

Don't let the sun go down on your anger, trust that God knows and will repay evil. Everything done in the dark will be exposed in the light.

Forgive. Jesus said if you forgive others, God will forgive you. Forgiveness is a gift for yourself, take it, accept it, use it, and live free.

Don't allow being offended ruin you or anyone else around you. Drop your offenses at the foot of the Cross where your debt was paid, and all your offenses were forgiven. Live free, unoffended, knowing the Lord is generous, kind, compassionate, loving, and eternally takes care of His children.

Whatever you believe the world owes you, remember God will supply all your needs. He is the provider and will give what you need for every step of your journey.

Keep doing good, for what you sow for God's kingdom will be eternally rewarded in God's kingdom. Live an honorable life, worthy of God by loving God and loving others.

The mercy of Jesus Christ took your punishment for all your offenses and all that you owed, so that you could live eternally free in the grace of His love.

His Present

Please read the following verses.

What does God say about taking revenge? Why is it necessary for us to forgive? What happens when we forgive others?

"Never take your own revenge, beloved, but leave room for the wrath of God, for it is written, 'Vengeance is Mine, I will repay,' says the Lord." ~ Romans 12:19 (NASB)

"For if you forgive others their sins, your heavenly Father will also forgive you. But if you do not forgive others, your Father will not forgive you your sins." ~ Matthew 6:14-15 (NET Bible)

"Be kind to one another, tender-hearted, forgiving each other, just as God in Christ also has forgiven you." ~ Ephesians 4:32 (NASB)

What happens if we allow a root of resentment to stay in our lives?

"Exercise foresight and be on the watch to look [after one another], to see that no one falls back from and fails to secure God's grace (His unmerited favor and spiritual blessing), in order that no root of resentment (rancor, bitterness, or hatred) shoots forth and causes trouble and bitter torment, and the many become contaminated and defiled by it." ~ Hebrews 12:15 (AMPC)

How as Christians are we to live our lives? Why?

"...live lives [of honor, moral courage, and personal integrity] worthy of the God who [saves you and] calls you into His own kingdom and glory. As Jesus said, "Love each other. Just as I have loved you, you should love each other. Your love for one another will prove to the world that you are my disciples." ~ 1 Thessalonians 2:12 (AMP), John 13:34-35 (NLT)

What promises do we have from God's word on His provision in working for Him? How many needs will God meet?

"God will supply all your needs according to His riches in glory in Christ Jesus. So let's not allow ourselves to get fatigued doing good. At the right

Present in His Presence

time we will harvest a good crop if we don't give up or quit. Right now, therefore, every time we get the chance, let us work for the benefit of all, starting with the people closest to us in the community of faith."~ Philippians 4:19 (NASB), Galatians 6:9-10 (MSG)

Love them to Life

A friend of mine has problems with the church. Growing up in church, Chris felt ostracized and excluded by other Christian kids. Because Chris didn't conform exactly to how other kids in the youth group acted and didn't listen to the "proper" Christian music, Chris was shunned.

Chris loves Jesus, loves God, is an adult now, but still has a challenging time getting back into church, because the church, and other Christian organizations, didn't have open arms. Shunning Chris in church, killed Chris' love for the church.

The fact grieves my heart. And to be honest, it grieves my heart because I remember times I've seen someone who didn't dress in the "proper" church attire or act like the rest of the churchgoers, and I was uncomfortable. I might have been polite, but I don't think I was that welcoming. I am so sorry.

I wonder if we think being rude to someone will get them to change. The behavior reminds me of the time I was a kid and acted silly, talked too much, and didn't have the money to wear fashionable clothes, and was shunned by others in school. I was hurt, and being shunned didn't help change me in positive ways.

Jesus didn't tell people to clean up their act before they came to Him. Jesus went to the sinners, the broken, the ostracized, the ones who didn't fit in with the religious. Jesus never shunned people, He loved them to life – His eternal life.

Let's not shun people, let's love people with the love of Jesus to point them to the love of Jesus. The love of a Savior, never shuns, but loves to Life.

His Present

How and why should we live as loving Christians?

"Little children (believers, dear ones), let us not love [merely in theory] with word or with tongue [giving lip service to compassion], but in action and in truth [in practice and in sincerity, because practical acts of love are more than words]." ~ 1 John 3:18 (AMP)

But God...

Ever wondered if you have gone too far from God's grace? Satan wants people to think because of sin and failures they are without hope. Thankfully, the Bible doesn't hide the imperfections of those listed as heroes of the faith.

David was an adulterer and murderer, but God called him a man after His own heart. Moses killed a man, but God spoke to him face-to-face as a friend. Rahab was a prostitute, but God blessed her to be in the lineage of Jesus Christ.

Peter denied Christ three times, but Jesus restored him. Paul persecuted Christians, but God saved Paul and used him in mighty ways to further His kingdom.

The Bible is full of examples of imperfect people—prostitutes, liars, adulterers, murderers, and thieves, but God forgave, restored and renewed their lives.

Even when you stumble and fall in sin, God makes whole through the grace, mercy, and forgiveness of Jesus' sacrifice.

His Present

Think of those listed in the Bible as great people of faith. God didn't hide their imperfections.

Which person or persons in the Bible do you most identify with? Why?

Consider how God redeemed their life and used them in mighty ways. Be encouraged that God's grace and forgiveness are also available for you.

Put your name in the following verse, "But God shows his love for us in that while we were still sinners, Christ died for us." ~ Romans 5:8 (ESV)

Thank God for all the ways He has forgiven and redeemed you.

Storm comfort

Overwhelmed with sadness for those affected by the storms of life, I grieved, prayed, and ran to God. My family lives in the Houston area, along with many friends, and during Hurricane Harvey there was so much heartache and pain.

Hurricanes, wildfires, shootings, and other heartache and tragedy keeps me in God's word for comfort in His love and mercy.

You too may be overwhelmed. Oh friend, even when terrible things happen, even when the flood of life overwhelms, God's mercies and comfort are there. God will not forsake you; He will not leave you; He will walk with you through the trials and suffering, and His love will safely carry you close to His heart.

Read the following verses for God's reassurance.

God hears and rescues. "Hear my cry, O God; give heed to my prayer. From the end of the earth I call to You when my heart is faint; lead me to the rock that is higher than I. Stretch forth Your hand from on high; rescue me and deliver me out of great waters... He sent from above, He took me, He drew me out of many waters." ~ Psalm 61:1-2 (NASB), Psalm 144:7 (NASB), 2 Samuel 22:17 (NKJV)

God will help you through. "Because he has loved Me, therefore I will deliver him; I will set him securely on high, because he has known My name. He will call upon Me, and I will answer him; I will be with him in trouble; I will rescue him and honor him. When you pass through the waters, I will be with you; and through the rivers, they will not overflow you.... For I know the plans I have for you, declares the Lord, plans to prosper you and not to harm you, plans to give you hope and a future." ~ Psalm 91:14-15 (NASB), Isaiah 43:2 (NASB), Jeremiah 29:11 (NIV)

God protects. "The name of the Lord is a strong tower; the righteous runs into it and is safe. Therefore, let everyone who is godly pray to You in a time when You may be found; surely in a flood of great waters they will not reach him." ~ Proverbs 18:10 (NASB), Psalm 32:6-7 (NASB),

God comforts. "Blessed be the God and Father of our Lord Jesus Christ, the Father of mercies and God of all comfort, who comforts us in all our affliction so that we will be able to comfort those who are in any affliction with the comfort with which we ourselves are comforted by God. He tends his flock like a shepherd: He gathers the lambs in his arms and carries them close to his heart; he gently leads those that have young. The Lord's lovingkindnesses indeed never cease, for His compassions never fail. They are new every morning; great is Your faithfulness. 'The Lord is my portion,' says my soul, 'Therefore I have hope in Him.'" ~ 2 Corinthians 1:3-4 (NASB), Isaiah 40:11 (NIV), Lamentations 3:22-24 (NASB)

His Present

As you read the verses used in this devotion, which ones stand out to you? Make note of the truths that give you hope and encouragement.

"Jesus Christ is not my security against the storms of life, but He is my perfect security in the storms. He has never promised me an easy passage, only a safe landing." ~ Annie Johnson Flint

Whatever you are going through, whatever troubles you for the future, always remember, "... that neither death, nor life, nor angels, nor principalities, nor things present, nor things to come, nor powers, nor height, nor depth, nor any other created thing, will be able to separate us from the love of God, which is in Christ Jesus our Lord." ~ Romans 8:38-39 (NASB)

Waving

Fall arrived on the calendar, yet the air remained warm. Trees with their still-green leaves swayed in the wind. Mesmerized, I sat under a tall oak tree and breathed deep of the beauty of God's nature. The gentle waving motion of the trees beckoned to bring focus up to the sky and up to God.

I wonder, how many times does God wave hope, joy, life, peace, and glory from the heavens to those of us living on planet earth? How often do we miss God's tender love? Flowers wave their petals at passers-by, birds wing and wave, the waves wave against the shore, as God reveals His glory. Stars twinkle in the night, winking and waving at the world.

Breathe deep, cease striving, be still, listen, watch, and see God's amazing glory waving love to you.

Heavenly Father, even in the business of the day, thank You that I can come to You for rest and refreshing. Thank You that even in the storms of life, Your constant glory shines from above. Still my soul in You. Still my soul to enjoy the waving of Your unfailing love from the heavens.

His Present

In what ways does nature call for people to notice God?

"The heavens are telling of the glory of God; and their expanse is declaring the work of His hands. Day to day pours forth speech, and night to night reveals knowledge." ~ Psalm 19:1-2 (NASB)

"The heavens declare His righteousness, and all the peoples have seen His glory." ~ Psalm 97:6 (NASB)

What does God ask us to do in the Psalm below? What promises does He declare?

"Be still and know (recognize, understand) that I am God. I will be exalted among the nations! I will be exalted in the earth. The Lord of hosts is with us; The God of Jacob is our stronghold [our refuge, our high tower]. Selah." ~ Psalm 46:10-11 (AMP)

Jesus tells us to come to Him. What happens when we do?

"Come to Me, all you who labor and are heavy-laden and overburdened, and I will cause you to rest. [I will ease and relieve and refresh your souls.] Take My yoke upon you and learn of Me, for I am gentle (meek) and humble (lowly) in heart, and you will find rest (relief and ease and refreshment and recreation and blessed quiet) for your souls." ~ Matthew 11:28-29 (AMPC)

Profitable

One morning while mentally whining about the lack of something in my life, this verse popped up for daily reading, "Thus says the Lord, your Redeemer, the Holy One of Israel, 'I am the Lord your God, who teaches you to profit, Who leads you in the way you should go.'" ~ Isaiah 48:17

The word "profit" stood out, so I looked up the word on the 1828 Shaffer's Dictionary (https://1828.mshaffer.com/) and highlighted words that applied to my situation.

Profit is literally to proceed forward, to advance; to urge or drive. In commerce, the advance in the price of goods sold beyond the cost of purchase. Any gain. Any advantage. The acquisition of anything valuable, corporeal or intellectual, temporal or spiritual. To profit one's self by reading or instruction. To make improvement; to grow wiser or better; to advance in anything useful. To be of use or advantage; to bring good to.

How exciting that God's profit is much bigger than we can even imagine. When God teaches us to profit, He is urging us forward for profitable improvement, advantage, advancement, to be of use for His purposes and His kingdom, leading in the way we should go. I love that!

Bible study is fun and exciting when we realize that every word is full of life and truth. The more we dig into God's word, ponder the deeper truths, the more we understand. God's Word unfolds like a blooming flower as we study and research.

His Present

When you look at the definition of profit in the devotion, what applies to your situation? In what ways has God made you profitable?

Based on the verses below, how do you make your soul prosperous

"Beloved, I pray that in all respects you may prosper and be in good health, just as your soul prospers." ~ 3 John 2 (NASB)

"This Book of the Law shall not depart out of your mouth, but you shall meditate on it day and night, that you may observe and do according to all that is written in it. For then you shall make your way prosperous, and then you shall deal wisely and have good success." ~ Joshua 1:8 (AMPC)

What's in your hand?

I didn't want to get out of bed. Even though I didn't have a reason to be depressed, depression had hit hard. Blessings abounded, yet one thing made me sad, one thing I longed for but didn't have.

Picking up my Bible, I read again where Moses first encountered God in the desert, where God called Moses to return to Egypt and lead the Israelites to freedom. Moses wasn't confident in his own abilities and wasn't sure the Israelites would believe God had sent him (see Exodus 3 – 4).

"The Lord said to him, 'What is that in your hand?' And he said, 'A staff'" (Exodus 4:2 NASB) Moses held a simple shepherd's staff, only a piece of wood, surely, he didn't have what was needed to go against Pharaoh and the armies of Egypt. However, God used Moses, and that simple piece of wood, in mighty ways to show God's power.

Far too often I've thought I didn't have what I needed, or know the right connections, or have the speaking ability, writing ability, ability in any ability, and I wasn't completing anything because I was so busy thinking I was missing something and in need of something. Ack!

Oswald Chambers wrote, "The first habit to form is the habit of realizing the provision God has made." Just as God asked Moses to look at what was in his hand, I need to open my eyes to see what God has already given.

Hmmm, so what is in my hand? I believe God has called me to write, that talent, that gifting, came from God, but I need to use what God has given. Instead of looking at my shortcomings, or anything I think I'm lacking, I need instead to focus on God and allow Him to use me in the ways He chooses.

Nothing is impossible for God; He is faithful to complete the work He began in us. It's not our might or our power but by His Spirit, giving strength, equipping, and empowering. He uses the weak to show His might, and He gives us all we need to complete what we are called to complete.

"The most healthy state of a Christian is always to be empty of self and constantly depending upon the Lord for provision; to be consistently poor in self and rich in Jesus; to be weak as water personally, but mighty through God to do great exploits."
~ C. H. Spurgeon

What has God given you? What is in your hand? Be who God created you to be, do what God called you to do, live, truly live your life in Christ and allow His power to work in you and through you.

His Present

What task do you feel God has asked you to complete?

Read the following verses. Where is power in the Christian life found? What kind of power is available to us as Christians?

"We have this treasure in clay jars, so that the extraordinary power belongs to God and does not come from us. ... The power that is working within us is able to do far beyond all that we ask or think."
~ 2 Corinthians 4:7, Ephesians 3:20 (NET)

Now, when you think about the task you have been given, where will you find the power needed, and how much power will be given?

Don't get under the wrong wing!

The media lumps people in categories by political party affiliation, race, and religion to divide and breed fear and mistrust. People are clumped into groups as left wing, right wing, or independent.

But you know what, whether you are left wing, right wing, independent, or a buffalo wing, the only wing to be under is God's wing. Only God speaks truth, He is the only One to follow, He is the only One who brings eternal safety and protection. Jesus Christ is the only Savior.

If you want to follow anyone, if you want to be under anyone's wing, please let it be Jesus Christ.

His Present

Under whose wing will you find safety and protection?

"How precious is Your lovingkindness, O God! And the children of men take refuge in the shadow of Your wings." ~ Psalm 36:7 (NASB)

"He will cover you with His pinions, and under His wings you may seek refuge; His faithfulness is a shield and bulwark." ~ Psalm 91:4 (NASB)

Humble prayers

Natural disasters, heartache, pain, and attacks happen around the globe, and the call for Christians to pray is echoing across our country and through social interactions. Many of you are facing disasters in your own lives. Tragedy hits us all and hits us hard, and we pray for our loved ones, lost ones, and hurting ones.

Most of us are familiar with the verse, "If My people who are called by My name will humble themselves, and pray and seek My face, and turn from their wicked ways, then I will hear from heaven, and will forgive their sin and heal their land. (2 Chronicles 7:14 NKJV)

The call to pray comes for those who are called by God's name, for those who seek His face, those who are His people. The call is for us to repent and humble ourselves before almighty God.

Andrew Murray wrote, "God can only reveal His will to a heart that is humble and tender and empty."

Oh, that our hearts would be contrite, humble, tender, and empty, kneeling before our Heavenly Father as we ask for His intervention for our loved ones, country, and world.

Humble prayers are powerful prayers.

Let's humbly kneel before God and ask for His tender mercies for our families, our country, and our world.

His Present

Please read the following verse. What kind of person is God looking for?

"Thus says the Lord, 'Heaven is My throne, and the earth is My footstool. Where then is a house you could build for Me? And where is a place that I may rest? For My hand made all these things, thus all these things came into being, declares the Lord. But to this one I will look, to him who is humble and contrite of spirit, and who trembles at My word.'" ~ Isaiah 66:1-3 (NASB)

When we come humbly to God, righteous by the blood of His Son, Jesus Christ, what will our prayers become?

"...The prayer of a righteous person is powerful and effective." ~ James 5:16 (NIV)

It will make a difference

Have you ever wondered if what you share about God has an impact for the Kingdom of God?

I have good news. When you speak or write God's word, when you share the good news message of Jesus Christ, it will make a difference, it will have an impact.

God's word travels through space and time, planting, growing, and harvesting for His kingdom. His word never returns void, it produces and prospers in the way He desires.

We might not see the difference with our earthly eyes, but we can be assured God's word always produces, prospers, and accomplishes beautiful results.

Keep sharing God's word, continue to read and study His Word so that you can speak His truth in love. You don't have to be a mighty theologian to make an impact in the world, every word you speak that is God's Word will make a difference and accomplish the purpose for which God desires.

If you have taken in the Good News and you spread that Good News, it will make a difference. And, when you speak and share God's Word, the harvest produced will be beyond your wildest dreams.

His Present

What promises are given when we share God's word?

"For as the rain and snow come down from the heavens, and return not there again, but water the earth and make it bring forth and sprout, that it may give seed to the sower and bread to the eater, so shall My word be that goes forth out of My mouth: it shall not return to Me void [without producing any effect, useless], but it shall accomplish that which I please and purpose, and it shall prosper in the thing for which I sent it. ~ Isaiah 55:10-11 (AMPC).

"The seed cast on good earth is the person who hears and takes in the News, and then produces a harvest beyond his wildest dreams." ~ Matthew 13:23 (MSG)

If you only knew...

If you only knew how much you are loved. If you only knew good things are coming. If you only knew I'm here for you, always here for you. If you only knew, you are never alone.

Lift up your eyes to see Me. Lift up your eyes to see the intricacies of My creation. I count the stars and know each one by name. I know the numbers of hairs on your head, the thoughts that run through your mind, your concerns, your worries, your hope and dreams, I know them all, and I love you.

My Son, Jesus Christ, died and rose again to save you so that you would always be with Me. Oh, if you only knew and could understand the depth of My love.

What you face today, I will be with you. What you faced in the past, I will heal and restore. What you face tomorrow, I will be with you. I know your name, I you are Mine.

Don't worry, don't be anxious, I am with you always to give you My peace, My comfort, My joy, and My strength.

Oh, if you only knew how much I love you! –
Love, *Your Heavenly Father*

Scripture reference: Psalm 33:18, Romans 8:28, Jeremiah 29:11, Isaiah 40:26, Isaiah 51:6, Luke 12:7, Psalm 94:11, John 3:16, Romans 8:39, Ephesians 3:17-19, Psalm 147:3, Isaiah 43:1, John 14:27, Isaiah 40:1, Isaiah 49:13, John 15:11, Isaiah 40:29, John 14:27, Psalm 33:5, Jeremiah 31:3

His Present

God's love is unfailing and everlasting. His ears are attentive to the cries of His children. When you read the promises from His word, make them personal, take them personally. God loves you forever and ever. Take time to thank God for His everlasting love.

"I have loved you with an everlasting love." ~ Jeremiah 31:3 (NASB)

"The eyes of the Lord are toward the righteous and His ears are open to their cry." ~ Psalm 34:15 (NASB)

"Our loving Lord is not just present, but nearer than the thought can imagine - so near that a whisper can reach Him." ~ Amy Carmichael

True knowledge

Ever gone to a friend for a listening ear and instead received advice that had nothing to do with your problem? Perhaps you didn't even want advice and just needed a hug.

People are limited in knowledge and often respond in a way they think is helpful but is not what was needed.

Since none of us have mind-reading skills, our sympathies and advice can be misconstrued and often miss the mark. Our advice and reactions are usually taken from our own life, what we've seen, heard, and experienced. Even taking college courses, reading books, attending seminars, and studying psychology, may make us wiser, but we can never have complete knowledge of another person.

Fortunately, Jesus knows our hearts and knows our thoughts. He knows precisely what is happening with us every moment of our days.

Jesus walked the dusty roads of earth, lived in human skin, and encountered the good, bad, and ugly of life. Jesus can sympathize with our weakness, He knows our frailties, and He knows our stories from beginning to end.

Jesus understands humanity and he understands us. We can be assured when we seek His counsel, we will find the exact mercy, grace, wisdom, and help we need.

His Present

The following verses are a description of Jesus. As you read, make the verse personal.

"Since then we have a great high priest who has passed through the heavens, Jesus, the Son of God, let us hold fast our confession. For we do not have a high priest who is unable to sympathize with our weaknesses, but one who in every respect has been tempted as we are, yet without sin. Let us then with confidence draw near to the throne of grace, that we may receive mercy and find grace to help in time of need." ~ Hebrews 4:14-16 (ESV)

Write the things troubling you. When you finish, take those items to God in prayer and confidently rest knowing that Jesus is lovingly interceding on your behalf.

Resonate

Sidetracked by the divisive negativity online and in the media, I felt out of balance and out of tune with God. Noise and distractions scream for attention, and trying to find a harmonious balance seems nearly impossible. Needing a soul tune-up, I ran to my office to read my Bible.

I've been a Christian for decades, yet verses and words will still seem to pop off the page. I can even have a verse underlined with notes beside the scripture, and as I read the verse again there will be a new truth that resonates in my soul.

Just as a tuning fork resonates with a pure musical tone, the correct pitch, the Holy Spirit resonates in our spirit to help tune in to God and His pure Truth.

The Holy Spirit is the Comforter, Counselor, Helper, Intercessor, Advocate, Strengthener, Standby, to teach us all things, the profound depths, divine counsel, the deep things of God.

Need a tune up and a tune in to God? God's word is Truth, and Jesus says the truth sets us free (John 8:32). Even in the noise and distractions, soul balance can be found in God.

Read God's word and ask the Holy Spirit to teach the things that will comfort you, counsel you, help you, intercede for you, advocate for you, strengthen you, and stand by you so that you may learn the deep things of God. Whatever is out of tune will be brought into correct pitch and pure harmony with the freedom found in the truth of God's word.

His Present

What does the Holy Spirit do for believers?

"The Helper (Comforter, Advocate, Intercessor—Counselor, Strengthener, Standby), the Holy Spirit, whom the Father will send in My name [in My place, to represent Me and act on My behalf], He will teach you all things. And He will help you remember everything that I have told you. For God has unveiled them and revealed them to us through the [Holy] Spirit; for the Spirit searches all things [diligently], even [sounding and measuring] the [profound] depths of God [the divine counsels and things far beyond human understanding]." ~ John 14:26 (AMP), 1 Corinthians 2:10 (AMP)

How does the Holy Spirit reassure you as a believer?

"For you have not received a spirit of slavery leading again to fear [of God's judgment], but you have received the Spirit of adoption as sons [the Spirit producing sonship] by which we [joyfully] cry, 'Abba! Father!' The Spirit Himself testifies and confirms together with our spirit [assuring us] that we [believers] are children of God." ~ Romans 8:15-16 (AMP)

In what ways does the Holy Spirit help and gift you?

"We also speak of these things, not in words taught or supplied by human wisdom, but in those taught by the Spirit, combining and interpreting spiritual thoughts with spiritual words [for those being guided by the Holy Spirit]. ... to each one is given the manifestation of the Spirit [the spiritual illumination and the enabling of the Holy Spirit] for the common good." ~1 Corinthians 2:13 (AMP), 1 Corinthians 12:7 (AMP)

Happy dancing from the rooftops

The world is going to hell in a handbasket. I've heard that terminology for years and it's often said with a sad sigh and usually given without any hope. It's true, Satan wants the world to go to hell in a handbasket, and he's out to steal, kill, and destroy. But I have good news, Jesus saves and gives eternal life.

We have been gifted The Good News to share the Good News about the Savior. "... whoever believes will in Him have eternal life. For God so loved the world, that He gave His only begotten Son, that whoever believes in Him shall not perish, but have eternal life. For God did not send the Son into the world to judge the world, but that the world might be saved through Him" (John 3:15-17 NASB).

The offer made through God's love, through the saving grace of Jesus, is GOOD NEWS! Accepting this gift isn't just fire insurance against hell, Jesus gives abundant life, joy, hope, and life eternal in paradise.

Let's make a difference. Let's celebrate, happy dancing from the rooftops to share the Good News about our wonderful Savior. Let's rise up to snatch the lost from the fire.

Let's live in such a way that people are drawn to the light of Christ shining within us. Let's march toward hell for a heavenly cause and spread the Good News – Jesus saves. Jesus is the life, the truth, and the way to eternal life and heaven.

I have Good News, we have Good News, Jesus saves, Jesus saves, Jesus saves!

His Present

According to the verses below, what joyful truths and gifts did God give you?

"For the wages of sin is death, but the free gift of God [that is, His remarkable, overwhelming gift of grace to believers] is eternal life in Christ Jesus our Lord." ~ Romans 6:23 (AMP)

"When God our Savior revealed his kindness and love, he saved us, not because of the righteous things we had done, but because of his mercy. He washed away our sins, giving us a new birth and new life through the Holy Spirit." ~ Titus 3:4-5 (NLT)

"By entering through faith into what God has always wanted to do for us—set us right with him, make us fit for him—we have it all together with God because of our Master Jesus. And that's not all: We throw open our doors to God and discover at the same moment that he has already thrown open his door to us. We find ourselves standing where we always hoped we might stand—out in the wide open spaces of God's grace and glory, standing tall and shouting our praise." ~ Romans 5:1-2 (MSG)

Staying silent

The other night, I dreamed I tried to get out of a tall building. I took the stairs, but they didn't go far. I tried an elevator, but it only went a few floors. I tried another stairway, and it also wouldn't take me out of the building. Finally, I found another elevator, and when the doors opened, some people came out, stared at me, and then accused me of saying things and doing things I didn't say or do. I stood stunned, I had no recourse, no way to prove they were wrong, there wasn't video proof, there wasn't anyone else who witnessed I didn't say or do those things.

When I awakened, I realized I had been overly cautious with what I post online and what I say, hoping to stay under the devil's radar. For years, I worried and tried hard to say the "right" things, do the "right" things, and be careful about everything, and anything, as I tried to please God and please men.

Pleasing God should be the goal, whereas pleasing people is always a snare (Proverbs 29:25). Since I worried too much about other people and what they thought, and what I thought they thought, I was often afraid to say a word.

Satan wants silent Christians, not talking about faith, or sin, or about Jesus Christ. Jesus calls us to speak the Truth in love, and speaking the truth is often met with negative results.

Even if I try to hide and be quiet about some things, there will be hostility, troubles will come because everyone who seeks to live a Godly life will be persecuted (2 Timothy 3:12).

My silence, my tiptoeing around certain issues, will not save me from Satan's hostility. My website stays under attack (over 1000 attacks on the day before I wrote this devotion). The devil is always trying to mess with me and my family. Jesus tells us not to fear, He has us safe in the palm of His loving hands, but that doesn't mean life will be without difficulty. We live in enemy territory.

I can hide what I think about some subjects, but that doesn't mean I'm doing the right thing or living in obedience to God. Staying silent only allows Satan freedom to continue in his devious plans. Satan wants to intimidate Christians to be silent about sin, so that people stay trapped in their sin. Sin is always destructive. The devil twists and manipulates to keep Christians and others fearful and silent.

When Jesus walked on this earth during His ministry, He went to those who were falling apart, weary, trapped in sin, who needed healing and hope. Jesus Christ came to seek and save the lost, He is the Way to new life and new beginnings.

Jesus' offer to accept His grace is so that He can give those who receive Him the absolute best – salvation, healing, restoration, joy, peace, love, and eternal life in paradise.

As a Christian, I have been given the honor and blessing of knowing Jesus Christ. I am to share with others who Jesus Christ is and how His love conquers sin and death. I will not stay silent. I will speak, write, and share about my wonderful Savior, His love, and His beautiful, amazing grace. "for we cannot stop speaking about what we have seen and heard." ~ Acts 4:20 (NASB)

His Present

Speaking about God and Jesus is not always met with positive results. However, what does God promise when we speak as Christians?

"...Do not be afraid any longer but go on speaking and do not be silent. ... Have I not commanded you? Be strong and courageous! Do not tremble or be dismayed, for the Lord your God is with you wherever you go." ~ Acts 18:9 (NASB), Joshua 1:9 (NASB)

"Here's a word you can take to heart and depend on: Jesus Christ came into the world to save sinners. I'm proof—Public Sinner Number One—of someone who could never have made it apart from sheer mercy. And now he shows me off—evidence of his endless patience—to those who are right on the edge of trusting him forever. Deep honor and bright glory to the King of All Time—One God, Immortal, Invisible, ever and always. Oh, yes!" ~ 1 Timothy 1:15-20 (MSG)

Finding Hope

My friend, downcast, broken, really didn't want to live. They wondered, what was the purpose in working hard when there wasn't any reward? What was the purpose in living a good life when everything around them was so bad? The world was imploding, people offended and exploding in anger. Why were they alive when there didn't seem to be any hope or purpose in them living?

Oh, my friend, you are part of something bigger. Your life makes a difference, you were birthed, placed, and given a purpose that makes an impact and plays a part in something amazing. It's not about now, it's not about the past, it's not about perception, or even what is seen with your eyes, you are made for eternity. And, eternity is alive, living, and real. You are part of something bigger, something beyond imagination, something so wonderful words can't describe.

Jesus is abundant life, full-joy, hope, peace, and purpose. You are given eternity, a never-rusting treasure, a mansion in paradise, everlasting life without pain, abundant never-ending life. While you are here on this earth, your purpose, every breath you are given, is for a beautiful reason.

I could write for years and tell you the people who came into my life, perhaps only for a second, who made an impact and kept me going. And, everyone you meet, every prayer you pray, every step you take, has an impact.

Satan wants you to think your life is small, insignificant, and without purpose. Oh, but let me tell you the truth, there is no one else like you on this planet, and without you the planet would not be the same.

We need you.

We need your prayers, your testimony, your smile, your encouragement, and even your failures can be used by God to show the grace of God. Oh, friend, it's so much bigger than you imagine. Your eternal soul is intertwined with the body of Christ that lives, and shines, and brings life in abundance.

Hope is here, now, eternal, beautiful, and wonderful. Hope breathes deep in your soul to encourage, bless, grow, motivate, and explode the joy of Christ within you. Your life is so much bigger than you imagine. Beyond your sight and your circumstances, amazing things are happening.

Keep going friend because your life is bigger than you imagine!

And now, I pray that the eyes of your heart may be enlightened, so that you will know and understand the hope of your calling, the immeasurable, unlimited, surpassing greatness of the power of Christ living within you, giving you strength, courage, comfort, and eternal hope.

"Hope forever, for God will not fail you!"
~ Charles Spurgeon

His Present

Paul prays that the eyes of our hearts will be enlightened to know the hope of our calling. According to the verses above, what amazing truths are you given as a believer in Christ?

"I pray that the eyes of your heart may be enlightened, so that you will know what is the hope of His calling, what are the riches of the glory of His inheritance in the saints, and [so that you can know and understand] what is the immeasurable and unlimited and surpassing greatness of His power in and for us who believe, as demonstrated in the working of His mighty strength. Now may our Lord Jesus Christ Himself and God our Father, Who loved us and gave us everlasting consolation and encouragement and well-founded hope through [His] grace (unmerited favor), comfort and encourage your hearts and strengthen them [make them steadfast and keep them unswerving] in every good work and word." ~ Ephesians 1:18 (NASB), Ephesians 1:19 (AMPC), 2 Thessalonians 2:16-17 (AMPC)

Small beginnings

The seemingly small and insignificant thing, the work God has called you to do behind the scenes, that doesn't seem to be of any worth, the Lord watches and rejoices to see the work begin.

Nothing is too small, for a tiny seed can produce a great harvest. Your step of obedience brings joy to the heart of God who watches and searches for those who will follow His will.

A small tribe of Israelites routed mighty armies and nations. For those who step out in faith, who follow God's leading, they step out in the power of God. A small boy brought a small meal to Jesus and that small meal fed thousands.

A widow tithed two small coins and her story has been told for generations. Small faith leads to great growth and amazing accomplishments.

Do not despise the small beginnings. What seems trivial to the world, may be the mighty move that sets in motion amazing changes in your life and in those around you.

No matter how small or insignificant it may seem, be diligent to complete the task God has called you to do, for small beginnings are the beginning of remarkable things.

His Present

"Do not despise these small beginnings, for the Lord rejoices to see the work begin, ..." ~ Zechariah 4:10 (NLT)

What task do you feel God has given you? When you think of God rejoicing at your work, how does that make you feel?

"Be willing to be only a voice, heard but not seen; a mirror whose surface is lost to view, because it reflects the dazzling glory of the sun; a breeze that springs up just before daylight, and says, 'The dawn! the dawn!' and then dies away. Do the commonest and smallest things as beneath His eye." — George Matheson

"Embrace this God-life. Really embrace it, and nothing will be too much for you... That's why I urge you to pray for absolutely everything, ranging from small to large. Include everything as you embrace this God-life, and you'll get God's everything." (Mark 11:22-24 MSG).

Knowing isn't enough

"You believe that God is one; you do well. Even the demons believe—and shudder!" ~ James 2:19 (ESV)

Knowing Jesus is the Son of God isn't enough. "In the synagogue there was a man possessed by a demon, an evil spirit. He cried out at the top of his voice, 'Ha! What do you want with us, Jesus of Nazareth? Have you come to destroy us? I know who you are—the Holy One of God!'" (Luke 4:33-34 NIV).

Knowledge doesn't save. Religion doesn't save. Being "good" doesn't save. Jesus is the key to eternal life and salvation. Jesus is the way and the truth and the life. No one comes to the Father except through Him (John 14:6).

Trying alternative routes doesn't save. "For God so greatly loved and dearly prized the world that He even gave up His only begotten (unique) Son, so that whoever believes in (trusts in, clings to, relies on) Him shall not perish (come to destruction, be lost) but have eternal (everlasting) life" (John 3:16 AMP).

Belief and faith open the door for relationship. Believing moves knowledge to the heart. "If you confess with your mouth that Jesus is Lord and believe in your heart that God raised him from the dead, you will be saved. For it is by believing in your heart that you are made right with God, and it is by confessing with your mouth that you are saved" (Romans 10:9-10 NLT).

The truth is amazing. The way is simple.

Believe.

Jesus stands at the door of your heart. Have you invited Him in?

His Present

"Here I am! I stand at the door and knock. If anyone hears my voice and opens the door, I will come in" ~ Revelation 3:20 (NIV)

Love held Jesus on the cross. Love rose Jesus from the grave, and Love offers grace, mercy, forgiveness, hope, and eternal life.

Please take a moment to make sure you don't only know about Jesus, but your heart has accepted Jesus as Savior.

You are loved

People fail us, frustrate us, disappoint us, leave us, and there are days we just need to know someone cares. I have good news. You are loved. God loves you.

You. Are. Loved. Exceedingly, abundantly, more than you can ask or imagine.

Jesus deemed each person so valuable that He laid down His own life to offer mercy, grace, and salvation. "For God so greatly loved and dearly prized the world that He [even] gave up His only begotten (unique) Son, so that whoever believes in (trusts in, clings to, relies on) Him shall not perish (come to destruction, be lost) but have eternal (everlasting) life" (John 3:16 AMP)

God's love isn't dependent on your action or inaction. God is love. He IS love. No matter what you think, how you feel, whatever your current situation, regardless of what people do or don't do, one thing remains – God's love is unfailing. Jesus will never leave you or forsake you. Always remember, you are loved! You are loved. You are loved. You are loved.

You are loved. You are loved. You are loved. You are loved. You are loved. You are loved. You are loved. You are loved. You are loved. You are loved. You are loved. You are loved.

His Present

Will you join me in praying from God's word to acknowledge the love of God?

God, thank You that in Your unfailing love You lead the people You have redeemed. You save by Your right hand those who take refuge in You from their foes. Thank You, Heavenly Father, that Your unfailing love surrounds those who trust in You. The earth is full of Your unfailing love. Your eyes are on those who fear You, on those whose hope is in Your unfailing love. How priceless is Your unfailing love, and we take refuge in the shadow of Your wings. Therefore, we will put our hope in the Lord, for with the Lord is unfailing love! (Exodus 15:13, Psalm 17:7, Psalm 32:10, Psalm 33:5, Psalm 33:18, Psalm 33:22, Psalm 36:7, Psalm 130:7)

I'm always here

Years ago, the company where my husband worked outsourced his facility and he was laid off. For 448 long, long, *long* days he searched for new employment. When work finally came, we gathered up two weeks' worth of clothes, my laptop, our dog, and headed north to Idaho. Ten months later, we were still waiting for our Texas house to sell.

Our temporary apartment was a blessing, but I missed my privacy. I missed a quiet room where I could shut the door and spend time writing and talking with God. I missed my books. I missed my stuff. I wanted a couch that didn't feel like it was stuffed with prairie dog pelts. I wanted things to be different, and I wanted to be settled. Yes, the pity party had hit with full abandon, and the whine mode clung to my shoulders like a wet rag, and, a wet whining Buffaloe is not a pretty picture.

With my million complaints, I tromped to the kitchen and poured a cup of coffee. Leaning against the counter, I pondered what really was behind my frustrations. Deep in my soul I wondered if I was accomplishing what God wanted me to accomplish?

Why was I so unsettled? And why didn't I feel like God was with me?

Then, in my soul the still small voice whispered, "***I'm always here.***"

Tears fell as all my complaints sloughed off and fell in a heap to the floor.

I should have known God would never leave.

During difficulties, unwanted life changes, and the craziness of the day, it's easy to allow the mind to whirl with frustrations, whines, and complaints. And, far too easy to wonder in hardships if something is missing, something that keeps us from feeling God is near.

Whining and complaining wasn't the answer for my unsettled soul. However, remembering God's truth, **<u>the truth</u>** that He will never leave or forsake us. **<u>The truth</u>** that Jesus said, "I am with you always even to the end of the age." **<u>The truth</u>** that God's love is unfailing.

The truth of any situation is found in God's truth.

You may feel as though you are all alone. Nothing could be further from the truth. God's promises of His presence, His unfailing love, comfort, hope, and peace abound throughout His word. God's hope, His presence, His love, is with you, even to the end of the age.

Thank You Father that You promise to never leave or forsake us. Thank You for loving me even when I'm a whining mess. Thank You that nothing is impossible for You. Help me to take my eyes off anything that takes my focus away from You.

Quiet my soul to hear Your voice and stand firm in Your loving Truth that You are always here.

His Present

Read the following verses and make note of God's promises. What gives you the most encouragement and hope?

"Why are you in despair, O my soul? And why have you become disturbed within me? **Hope in God**, for I shall again praise Him for **the help of His presence**." ~ Psalm 42:5 (NASB)

"...the eyes of the Lord are on those who fear him, on those whose hope is in his **unfailing love**." ~ Psalm 33:18 (NIV)

"And the Lord, He is the One who goes before you. **He will be with you, He will not leave you nor forsake you**; do not fear nor be dismayed." ~ Deuteronomy 31:8 (NKJV)

"... "**Do not fear**, for I have redeemed you; I have called you by name; **you are Mine**! When you pass through the waters, **I will be with you**; and through the rivers, they will not overflow you. When you walk through the fire, you will not be scorched, nor will the flame burn you. For **I am the Lord your God**, The Holy One of Israel, your Savior..." ~ Isaiah 43:1-3 (NASB)

"... **I am with you always**, even to the end of the age." ~ Matthew 28:20 (NASB)

(Emphasis added on scripture.)

Worth it

You, the one with the hurting heart, who doesn't want to move forward, who doesn't want to risk loving again. Oh friend, it's worth the risk, the hurt, the pain. Though you feel like the walking dead, it's worth keeping your zombie heart beating.

Jesus is for you, loves you, wants you to trust Him. It's worth it to trust your heart to The One who made your heart, for Jesus heals broken hearts, He binds wounds. And He doesn't just heal and bind, He restores and makes new.

Jesus died, was buried, and three days later rose again so that you could live. His resurrected life will resurrect you.

Keep going, it's worth it to see what rises from the ashes, what is birthed from the darkest moments, what rises from the grave. With Jesus on your side, it's worth keeping going, it's worth it, always worth it.

One day everything will make sense, the greater purpose will be revealed, and every, ***every*** tear will be lovingly wiped away.

His Present

Keep going. For one day soon, so very soon... God Himself will rise with healing on His wings and wipe away every tear from your eyes; and there will no longer be any death; there will no longer be any mourning, or crying, or pain; the first things will pass away, and He will make all things new (Malachi 4:2, Revelation 21:3-5).

It's not what you think

Enjoying the day, sweet hubby and I made our way along a pathway in the woods. We stopped at a small bridge leading over a dry creek bed to survey the beauty. Sunlight filtered through the trees and their leaves swayed in the fall breeze.

Crashing sounds drew our attention to the woods. We expected to see a large animal or person running toward us. Instead, two chipmunks leaped and frolicked in the fallen leaves as they traveled to their destination. Shaking our heads in disbelief, we laughed at the tiny creatures making the big sounds. With that much noise, chipmunks were not what we expected.

Difficulties, hardship, pain, and challenges have roared and crashed into my life, and I (and others) expected the outcome to be different. If I followed what the world said about the things I have been through (molestation, rape, cancer, chronic illness, numerous surgeries, thirty-six moves, and a long list of nasty things), I should be sitting in a corner unable to function. But with God, it's not what you think, because with God, the mess becomes the ministry, and the test becomes the testimony.

What sounded like, seemed like, wasn't what was expected, because God turns everything into good for those who love Him and are called according to His purpose.

With God, nothing is impossible. The situations we go through, the things we see and experience, the terrible noise of our lives being upturned and overturned, are turned into good, healed, restored, and made new by God's love.

Our world is filled with sounds that distract, depress, and deflate our strength and stamina. Satan is like a roaring lion, and boy, can he roar. The enemy wants you to hear that things will never be fixed, never be right, and never be restored. However, I have good news -- Satan may roar like a lion, but our Savior is the Lion of Judah!

The sound of God's truth is louder, truer, and surer, than any noise in the world. God's truth is greater and exceedingly abundantly more than you could ask or imagine.

God's voice whispers in your soul and roars the truth of His tender, compassionate, unfailing love.

His Present

What truths are available for those who follow God, who listen for His voice?

"Righteousness and justice are the foundation of Your throne; lovingkindness and truth go before You. How blessed are the people who know the joyful sound! O Lord, they walk in the light of Your countenance. In Your name they rejoice all the day, and by Your righteousness they are exalted." ~ Psalm 89:14-16 (NASB)

"Then I heard something like the voice of a great multitude and like the sound of many waters and like the sound of mighty peals of thunder, saying, 'Hallelujah! For the Lord our God, the Almighty, reigns." ~ Revelation 19:6 (NASB)

"The voice of the Lord is powerful, the voice of the Lord is majestic. ...And in His temple everything says, 'Glory!'" ~ Psalm 29:4, 11 (NASB)

Soul-rehydration

I love reading the Bible, working through Bible studies, and reading books and posts about God. When I study, there are so many nuggets of truth I find along the way, and I can't wait to get online and share.

However, I stayed so busy, so distracted by social media, that my soul felt like a shriveled raisin. I needed to get back in the True Vine and be re-hydrated in The Living Water. I needed to saturate myself in God's Word, spend time with God, abide with Him, linger long and deep in His presence.

Jesus said He is the vine and those who abide in Him will bear much fruit (John 15:5). I want to abide in Christ and bear much fruit, I want to be like a big, juicy, fat grape on the vine of Christ. I can't do it on my own. I have nothing lasting to offer, that is worthy of lasting, if what I share doesn't come from God.

I believe my calling is to write and share God's truth, but when things were out of whack. I quietly stepped away from social media for a season. I didn't know how long (days, weeks, months, ...) or how things would look when God opened the door to return.

To be honest, I tried many times to step away, and I always ran back thinking someone needed me (ha!) or I wanted to share something that spoke to me, or I'm just way too curious about what's happening online.

Kelly Minter shared at the 2017 LifeWay Women's Leadership Forum, *"Those we minister to, don't need us to be busy for them, they need us to be in intimacy with Christ."*

I need Christ's intimacy, you need Christ's intimacy. We need to care for our souls and the soul-connection with God. We need to stay still, sit still long enough for God's truth to resonate, marinate, and re-hydrate our souls.

God calls, calls for you to come to Him, come and be still, and rest in His presence. In the vine of Christ, you find His love and His abundant fruit.

His Present

Is your soul weary and in need of refreshment? What does Jesus say will happen when you come to Him and when you abide in Him?

"Come to Me, all you who labor and are heavy-laden and overburdened, and I will cause you to rest. [I will ease and relieve and] refresh your souls.] Take My yoke upon you and learn of Me, for I am gentle (meek) and humble (lowly) in heart, and you will find rest (relief and ease and refreshment and recreation and blessed quiet) for your souls." ~ Matthew 11:28-29 (AMPC)

"I am the true vine, and My Father is the vinedresser. Every branch in Me that does not bear fruit, He takes away; and every branch that bears fruit, He prunes it so that it may bear more fruit. You are already clean because of the word which I have spoken to you. Abide in Me, and I in you. As the branch cannot bear fruit of itself unless it abides in the vine, so neither can you unless you abide in Me. I am the vine, you are the branches; he who abides in Me and I in him, he bears much fruit, for apart from Me you can do nothing." ~ John 15:1-5 (NASB)

I don't understand

I don't understand the evil in the world, the heartache, tragedy, and terrible things that happen. I don't understand the meanness of people. I don't understand illness that strikes innocent babies and children. I don't understand so many things that frustrate and leave me reeling and heartsick.

I don't understand...

But I do know God is good, He is just and righteous, He is compassionate and merciful. I know God is loving and even beyond loving because He is love and loves with unfailing love. I know that God will one day make all things right, that evil will be punished, and life will be restored into eternal life.

I don't understand, I can't understand many things, but I can stand on the truth of God. And, someday soon everything will make sense, and all will be made right. God will destroy evil, and those who love God, follow His Son Jesus Christ will be in paradise.

God Himself will wipe away every tear from our eyes. Death will not exist, and there will no longer be mourning, or crying, or pain, and all will be made new.

Heavenly Father, I don't understand so many things and so many days it's hard to stand. But, I will stand on the truth of Your unfailing love. Thank You that one day everything will make sense and You will make everything right and all right.

His Present

Understanding the things that happen, the heartache and pain in this world is difficult. We can't see the big picture, but we can be assured one day, all will become clear in the light of our Father's love.

"From the end of the earth I call to You when my heart is faint; lead me to the rock that is higher than I. For You are my rock and my fortress; for Your name's sake You will lead me and guide me."

"For the Lord is good. His loyal love endures, and he is faithful through all generations. The Lord is merciful and compassionate; he is patient and demonstrates great loyal love."

"God will take away all their tears. There will be no more death or sorrow or crying or pain. All the old things have passed away." Scripture reference: Psalm 61:2 (NASB), Psalm 31:3 (NASB), Psalm 100:5 (NET Bible), Psalm 145:8 (NET Bible) Revelation 21:4New Life Version (NLV)

Known

I want to be known. I want someone to know my heart. Oh, to be noticed, known, and loved.

Jesus said He knows His own and His own know Him. His sheep hear His voice, and He knows them, and they follow Him. When we are known by Jesus, we are known by the Father.

These truths make my heart leap with joy. As we give our hearts to Jesus, our hearts are opened to know Jesus, to know God, and to be eternally loved.

We don't have to search for God's heart, He promises, "I will give them a heart to know Me, for I am the Lord; and they will be My people, and I will be their God, for they will return to Me with their whole heart."

You may feel unnoticed and unloved, but the truth is God notices you, knows you, and loves you.

God sees you. He lovingly knit you together in your mother's womb, He knows the number of your days and wants to be with you all your days throughout all eternity.

God longs to live in your heart so that your heart knows Him and loves Him, as He eternally knows and loves you.

You are so known and so loved!

His Present

What promises does Jesus give in the following verses?

"I am the good shepherd, and I know My own and My own know Me. My sheep hear my voice, and I know them, and they follow Me... If one loves God truly [with affectionate reverence, prompt obedience, and grateful recognition of His blessing], he is known by God [recognized as worthy of His intimacy and love, and he is owned by Him]."

"This is eternal life, that they may know You, the only true God, and Jesus Christ whom You have sent."

Scripture Reference: John 10:14 (NASB), John 10:27 (NASB), John 17:3 (NASB) Jeremiah 24:7 (NASB), 1 Corinthians 8:3 (AMPC)

Heart attack

Heart attack warning! Our hearts are under attack; Satan wants our hearts to stop beating passionately for Christ. Don't let the enemy win. Put up heart guards. Proverbs 4:20-24 tells us we can guard our hearts by listening to God's word and keeping wisdom we learn through God's truth.

To keep hearts guarded, we must be careful what we watch, what we listen to, who we listen to, and what our mind dwells upon. The Bible is our offensive weapon against the enemy. God's word is the sword of truth that slashes away every enemy lie.

You are never alone in your battles. When battling (with the enemy, with life, with yourself), run to the Bible, read God's Word and say the Word. Go to God with every request, because God is more than a safe place to run, God is a defender and protector of His children. He is your shield.

Paul reminds us in Philippians 4:6-7 not to worry or be anxious but to bring every request to God with prayer and thanksgiving. The result is the peace of God beyond understanding which will guard our hearts and minds.

Psalm 91 has been one of my favorite refuge chapters, a place to read and hide in the shadow of God's wings, curled up safe and out of the battle.

However, during a spiritual battle, I realized Psalm 91 is much more. The verses are a fortress of safety in the heat of war, reminding us of the invincibility of those who abide in God's presence – life delivered, not from trouble, but life delivered in the midst of trouble.

Read for yourself Psalm 91 and see the richness of His truth to help on your journey. God's word is alive and active. As you dig into the Bible, you find more treasure. As your life moves forward, God's Word continues to flow into your ever-flowing life. Jesus is the Living Water. He is The Life, The Way, and The Truth, showing you the way to truly live.

You are precious to God and He cherishes His possessions. Guard your heart where Jesus lives. He is holy and He will help you live in His holiness. Guard closely the gift of His presence that lives within you.

Stand firm, stand up, put on your armor, grab your sword of the Spirit, which is the sword of Truth, fight and allow God to fight for you. Rely on God's power and might and His life will again breathe life.

His Present

What do the verses implore you to do? What promises are given when doing as advised?

"Dear friend, listen well to my words; tune your ears to my voice. Keep my message in plain view at all times. Concentrate! Learn it by heart! Those who discover these words live, really live; body and soul, they're bursting with health. Keep vigilant watch over your heart; that's where life starts." ~ Proverbs 4:20-23 (MSG)

Following

Social interactions can bring blessings or curses. When you "follow" someone on Facebook or Twitter, you can see their posts on the social feeds. There are those who post uplifting, Biblical, humorous, or thought-provoking material. Unfortunately, there are others who tend to use their pages to share political or divisive, negative information.

Fortunately, I have a choice who I follow. I can be friends with many people, but that doesn't mean I should listen to everyone's opinion or get sucked into the latest political drama. I need to be careful with what I watch and what I read. Therefore, I can quietly control what comes rolling through the news feed on the social sites by not following some people.

First and foremost, I follow God and His Son, Jesus Christ. Jesus said, "Follow Me." And, that is Who I will follow. Following Jesus isn't the popular route these days, but following Jesus is the only way to heaven, eternal life, and truly living while we are here on earth.

In your daily life and in your social interactions, make sure to follow those who won't distract or detract you from following Jesus Christ.

His Present

Jesus said, "Follow Me." (Matthew 4:19)

Follow Jesus, for He is the Life that leads to life. Jesus is The Way that will lead you along your way. Jesus is The Truth that will guide you in all truth. Jesus is the Prince of Peace that will lead you in peace.

Follow Jesus, for His is all in all.

My prayer for you... "I ask—ask the God of our Master, Jesus Christ, the God of glory—to make you intelligent and discerning in knowing him personally, your eyes focused and clear, so that you can see exactly what it is he is calling you to do, grasp the immensity of this glorious way of life he has for his followers, oh, the utter extravagance of his work in us who trust him—endless energy, boundless strength!" ~ Ephesians 1:17-19 (MSG)

What was done

What was done to me in my past by others — the sins they committed against me, the wrong done by them against me...

What was done by me — the sins I committed, the wrong turns I made...

What was done is replaced by what was done on the cross by Jesus Christ. Through Jesus, what was done is healed, restored, forgiven, and renewed.

What was done is made new by The One who says, "I am the Alpha and the Omega. I am the One who is and was and is coming. I am the Almighty" (Revelation 1:8 NCV).

What was done then, what was done before, becomes what is now – grace, mercy, healing, and eternal life.

His Present

Heavenly Father, thank You for Your Son, Jesus Christ. Thank You for the mercy through the cross. Thank You for forgiving me of my sins.

Thank You for Your grace and unfailing love that heals, restores, and wipes away every tear from what was done. God will create new heavens and a new earth; and the former things will not be remembered or come to mind.

He will wipe away every tear from our eyes; and there will no longer be any death; there will no longer be any mourning, or crying, or pain; the first things have passed away. ~ Isaiah 65:17 (NASB), Revelation 21:4 (NASB)

Fight the good fight

Tossing and turning in the night, I prayed, begged, and whined about a situation in a friend's life. I want things to be different for my friend, I want them to have peace and joy.

Oh, I know I should trust God. I know He is in control. I know God loves my friend more than I can imagine, yet my restless night continued.

I finally fell into sleep and had a dream about my friend. I could see something going on in their life, something not right. A man talking with my friend acted like he had positive intentions, but I knew deep in my spirit something was wrong, and I approached the man and told him I would do something to him, something very bad, if he hurt my friend. The man backed away and left.

I woke and realized I can do more for my friend. Worrying doesn't do anything positive for anyone. Prayer is a powerful, offensive weapon. I should continue praying, and I also need to stand against the enemy, and remember that God's Word is the ultimate offensive weapon.

I quietly got out of bed and went to another room and spoke God's truth out loud. I spoke the truth that Jesus has all authority in heaven and earth, and as a believer, one who follows Jesus as Lord, in the authority of Jesus Christ I can speak against the enemy.

God never leaves us defenseless in our battles. We are more than conquerors through Jesus Christ.

Charles Spurgeon wrote, "Herein is true wisdom. If you would successfully wrestle with Satan, make the Holy Scriptures your daily resort. Out of this sacred magazine continually draw your armor and your ammunition. Lay hold upon the glorious doctrines of God's Word; make them your daily meat and drink. So shall you be strong to resist the devil, and you shall be joyful in discovering that he will flee from you."

Therefore, we don't need to idly sit by whining, crying, and moaning about worries and fears. Our battles are beyond flesh and blood, and we fight in the heavenly realm for ourselves, for our family and friends, and for the lost.

God has not given the spirit of fear, we are given power (HIS power), love (unfailing love), and a sound mind (a mind that can trust and rest in God).

Put on your armor and stand against the enemy. Fight the good fight, take your concerns to God in prayer. Read, meditate, and speak God's Word to battle against Satan. The weapons of our warfare are mighty in God's power.

God's truth breaks apart strongholds and smacks down any argument, any lies of the enemy, and anything that exalts itself over the knowledge of God.

When those worries come, take the thoughts captive, wrap the lies of the enemy, the attacks of Satan, in the truth of God's Word. and The Truth will set you free.

His Present

God blesses us with His Word to guide and direct our daily lives. The more scripture we read and know, the more power we realize we have been given in the battles for ourselves and others.

Why is knowing God's word important?

"and you will know the truth, and the truth will set you free." ~ John 8:32 (NET Bible)

Please read the following verses. What power has Jesus been given? What has God given us through Jesus Christ?

"Jesus came and said to them, 'All power has been given to Me in heaven and on earth.'" ~ Matthew 28:18 (NLV)

"Praise be to the God and Father of our Lord Jesus Christ. In Christ, God has given us every spiritual blessing in the heavenly world." ~ Ephesians 1:3 (NCV)

"And He raised us up together with Him [when we believed], and seated us with Him in the heavenly places, [because we are] in Christ Jesus, Ephesians 2:6 (AMP)

How do we fight?

"Fight the good fight of faith. Take hold of the life that lasts forever. You were chosen to receive it. ..." 1 Timothy 6:12 New Life Version (NLV)

"Put on the full armor of God so that you can fight against the devil's evil tricks. Our fight is not against people on earth but against the rulers and authorities and the powers of this world's darkness, against the spiritual powers of evil in the heavenly world. That is why you need to put on God's full armor. Then on the day of evil you will be able to stand strong. And when you have finished the whole fight, you will still be standing." ~ Ephesians 6:11-13 (NCV)

"We are human, but we don't wage war as humans do. We use God's mighty weapons, not worldly weapons, to knock down the strongholds of human reasoning and to destroy false arguments. We destroy every proud obstacle that keeps people from knowing God. We capture their rebellious thoughts and teach them to obey Christ." ~ 2 Corinthians 10:3-5 (NLT)

What promises are we given as Christians?

"Yet amid all these things we are more than conquerors and gain a surpassing victory through Him Who loved us." ~ Romans 8:37 (AMPC)

"For God did not give us a spirit of timidity (of cowardice, of craven and cringing and fawning fear), but [He has given us a spirit] of power and of love and of calm and well-balanced mind and discipline and self-control." ~ 2 Timothy 1:7 (AMPC)

How much power are we given through prayer?

"The prayer from the heart of a man right with God has much power." ~ James 5:16 (NLV)

May our lives testify... "I have fought the good fight, I have finished the course, I have kept the faith." ~ 2 Timothy 4:7 (NASB)

Grudge nursing

Ever held a grudge? According to the dictionary a grudge is a persistent feeling of ill will or resentment resulting from a past insult or injury. Grudges are common, way too common.

With social interactions, fake news, agenda-driven media, and the ease of spreading opinions, someone is always feeding the flames to keep grudges growing and well-fed.

A grudge can seem harmless, maybe even seem like a little thing, but a grudge is like nursing a fifty-ton elephant that is going to squish the life out of your life.

Don't nurse a grudge, for grudges hold you in, entangle, enmesh, and subject you to their nasty temperaments.

Don't feed grudges, don't nourish grudges, don't allow grudges to grow. Nursing a grudge can lead to physical and mental consequences.

The bigger the grudge, the more they suck away your life, the more they affect those around you, and the less life you will be able to live.

Don't nurse a grudge, for a grudge grows into unforgiveness, which shackles you in ways that have very, very negative spiritual consequences.

Jesus said, "If you forgive those who sin against you, your heavenly Father will forgive you. But if you refuse to forgive others, your Father will not forgive your sins." ~ Matthew 6:14-15 (NLT)

Don't nurse a grudge because grudges are the devil's playground. "When angry, do not sin; do not ever let your wrath (your exasperation, your fury or indignation) last until the sun goes down. Leave no [such] room or foothold for the devil [give no opportunity to him]." ~ Ephesians 4:26-27 (AMPC)

Don't nurse a grudge, trust God. Trust God to do what is right. "Do not seek revenge or bear a grudge against anyone among your people but love your neighbor as yourself. I am the Lord." ~ Leviticus 19:18 (NIV)

For your freedom, for your blessings, for the blessings of others around you, don't nurse a grudge.

His Present

"Don't seek revenge or carry a grudge against any of your people. Love your neighbor as yourself. I am God." ~ Leviticus 19:18 (MSG)

"If it is possible, as far as it depends on you, live at peace with everyone. Do not take revenge, my dear friends, but leave room for God's wrath, for it is written: 'It is mine to avenge; I will repay,' says the Lord." ~ Romans 12:18-19 (NIV)

"Be kind to one another, tender-hearted, forgiving each other, just as God in Christ also has forgiven you." ~ Ephesians 4:32 (NASB)

Reflectors

A friend of mine wonders and worries about their purpose in life, what they are supposed to do, and how they can make an impact in the world. As I pondered how to respond, I thought of something that sits in our yard.

On one side of our property is a drain for street runoff. Because of the drainage area, our driveway has an odd angle at the end. To warn drivers to make proper adjustments before exiting, we placed a tall reflector about six feet from the street. That little reflector may not seem like much, yet that reflector redirects drivers to keep them from damaging the drainage area and/or their vehicle.

Reflectors have purpose, for safety they reflect light to direct, warn, and caution. As Christians, we are to reflect the light of Christ. Jesus said, "You are the light of the world. ... let your light shine before people, so that they can see your good deeds and give honor to your Father in heaven." (Matthew 5:14-16 NET Bible)

Wondering and worrying about my purpose has many times kept me from fulfilling my purpose. I often make life much harder than it has to be. Jesus said, "Love the Lord your God with all your heart, with all your soul, and with all your mind. This is the first and greatest commandment." (Matthew 22:37-38 NET Bible)

Our purpose is to love God, and the more we love God, the more brightly His glorious light shines within us.

As we go about each day, as we complete the tasks that need completing, as we encounter people along the way, let's reflect the light of Christ so that others (before they exit this world) will be directed to the light of Christ for eternal safety.

His Present

Who are you in Christ? "You are a chosen race, a royal priesthood, a holy nation, a people for God's own possession, so that you may proclaim the excellencies of Him who has called you out of darkness into His marvelous light" ~ 1 Peter 2:9 (NASB)

What message are you to proclaim? "Remember, our Message is not about ourselves; we're proclaiming Jesus Christ, the Master. All we are is messengers, errand runners from Jesus for you. It started when God said, 'Light up the darkness!' and our lives filled up with light as we saw and understood God in the face of Christ, all bright and beautiful. ... We are transfigured much like the Messiah, our lives gradually becoming brighter and more beautiful as God enters our lives and we become like him." ~ 2 Corinthians 4:5-6, 2 Corinthians 3:18 (MSG)

Casting

While reading in Exodus about the building of the tabernacle, I pondered a workman casting metal into a fire and creating something beautiful and new. Casting recreates.

Peter tells us to cast our care upon the Lord for He cares for us (1 Peter 5:7). Casting is to throw upon, place upon, and give up to God. A visual for me is to take my burdens to God and throw them upon His strong shoulders (and tie it to His altar so I can't get it back).

Casting brings peace. As we cast our worries and concerns on God, He restores what the enemy meant for evil, He makes all things beautiful in His time, He works all things for good, for nothing is impossible for Him.

God cares for you; you can trust His unfailing love. Casting your cares on God is a gift. Cast your burdens on the Lord and the weight will roll off your shoulders and onto God's strong, loving, all-powerful shoulders. Fear will be cast out and your mind and soul can rest in His peace.

His Present

As you rest in God's perfect love, what do you find? What happens when you release your burden to God? "There is no fear in love; but perfect love casts out fear." Therefore, "Cast your burden on the Lord [releasing the weight of it] and He will sustain you; He will never allow the [consistently] righteous to be moved (made to slip, fall, or fail)." ~ 1 John 4:18 (NKJV), Psalm 55:22 (AMPC)

The worst thing

What if you knew the worst thing, the very worst thing in your life, would lead to something amazing for you and for others?

The worst thing can be the best thing. Like Joseph told his brothers in Genesis 50:20 "you intended to harm me, but God intended it for good to accomplish what is being done, the saving of many lives."

We only see through human eyes, through our own filters, and our own hopes and dreams. We can't see the unseen, what will happen in the future, which way the journey will lead, but God knows. The relationship that God seemed to block was blocked to keep you from more heartache. The "no" God gave you, was because He had better for you.

Many of the worst things in my life have been used by God to bring comfort, hope, and healing to others. The messy, hard, heart-breaking, soul-crushing difficulties, became the best things as God healed and restored me and then used them to minister to others in His loving name.

Every problem is an opportunity to discover more of God and His power. Trials try and test us until we are refined and shine forth in God's healing, restoration power. Setbacks provide a step up to step closer to God, His Word, and His truth.

Take your worst thing to God in prayer, give it to God, sacrifice it on His altar with praise (trusting, knowing) that God works all things for good for those who love Him and are called according to His purpose (Romans 8:28). The One who died and rose again, will rise with new life for you. If you are God's child, He will take that thing, that very worst thing, and turn it into something new and amazing!

His Present

What promises do you have as you move forward with God?

"The Lord says, 'Forget what happened before, and do not think about the past. Look at the new thing I am going to do. It is already happening. Don't you see it? The One who was sitting on the throne said, 'Look! I am making everything new!' For you who fear my name, the Sun of Righteousness will rise with healing in his wings. And you will go free, leaping with joy like calves let out to pasture" ~ Isaiah 43:18-19 (NCV), Revelation 21:5 (NCV), Malachi 4:2 (NLT)

Light us up!

While praying for a friend's upcoming ministry conference, in my spirit I could "see" a dark place, a place with much opposition. I felt there was much hard ground to navigate, much darkness, but as I prayed I could "see" a crack in the earth, a dark crack opening and the opposition falling in. Then, God's light came blazing forth from the crack getting brighter and brighter as the crack grew wider and wider. God's light shone through the building and beyond, moving among houses, moving among the street, moving into the city, the state, and beyond. The more the prayers, the more the light continued to grow.

James tells us that "The heartfelt and persistent prayer of a righteous man (believer) can accomplish much [when put into action and made effective by God—it is dynamic and can have tremendous power] (James 5:16).

We are giving the gift and blessing of coming to our all-powerful God with our requests. Prayer is unstoppable in the unstoppable might of God.

Your prayers make a difference because nothing is impossible for God, and nothing can stop His light from shining.

"The prayer of the feeblest saint on earth who lives in the Spirit and keeps right with God is a terror to Satan. The very powers of darkness are paralyzed by prayer." ~ Oswald Chambers

Pray and watch God's light shine. He "desires all men to be saved and to come to the knowledge of the truth (1 Timothy 2:4), and when we pray for God's light to shine in a dark world, we are praying in accordance to His will.

In the Light, darkness must flee. No situation, no person, no demon is too dark for the light of Christ to dispel the darkness. Will you join me in praying for God's light to shine bright and move, move, move, move among the nations?

Light up Your people, Lord. Light them with Your light. Light them up with Your love to spread Your light among the nations.

Light us up, Lord!

Light us up with Your glory so that we may shine for You!

Light us up, Lord!

Please, light us up!

His Present

Jesus said, "I am the Light of the world; he who follows Me will not walk in the darkness but will have the Light of life." ~ John 8:12 (NASB)

As a Christian your way is lit by The Light of the World to bring His light to the world.

"For God, who said, 'Light shall shine out of darkness,' is the One who has shone in our hearts to give the Light of the knowledge of the glory of God in the face of Christ." ~ 2 Corinthians 4:6 (NASB)

"For you are all children of light, children of the day. We are not of the night or of the darkness."

"You are a chosen race, a royal priesthood, a holy nation, a people for God's own possession, so that you may proclaim the excellencies of Him who has called you out of darkness into His marvelous light" ~ 1 Thessalonians 5:5 (ESV), 1 Peter 2:9 (NASB)

Walk in the Light of Christ, keep praying and keep proclaiming the Light of Christ.

Fast-food

I spent way too much time on social sites, reading, interacting, and sharing snippets others had shared. At night, I crawled into bed with my soul feeling hurried and unsatisfied. I realized, instead of lingering slow, pondering, soaking, diving deep into God's Word, I had been looking for bites, fast-food morsels to nibble and parcel out to others. No wonder my soul was shriveled and unfulfilled.

In Jeremiah 2:5 God said the Israelites had been seeking after empty, and they became empty. Only God can satisfy a weary, hungry soul. Jesus declared, "I am the bread of life. Whoever comes to me will never go hungry, and whoever believes in Me will never be thirsty. And, blessed are those who hunger and thirst for righteousness, for they will be filled" (John 6:35, Matthew 5:6). Jesus is The Way to find true, live-giving, soul satisfaction.

The God of eternity beckons our hearts to come aside, rest awhile, to be still and know that He is God. Deep calls to deep, iron sharpens iron, and as our souls draw near to God, He draws near filling us with His eternal wisdom, life, peace, and joy.

The time God has given, the blessings He has provided, are to be used in ways that bless our souls. "Why do you spend money for that which is not bread, and your earnings for what does not satisfy? Listen carefully to Me, and eat what is good, and let your soul delight in abundance. For I satisfy the weary ones and refresh everyone who languishes (Isaiah 55:2, Jeremiah 31:25).

As you spend time in God's presence, you find, "the Lord will continually guide you, and satisfy your desire in scorched places, and give strength to your bones; and you will be like a watered garden, and like a spring of water whose waters do not fail. For He has satisfied the thirsty soul, and the hungry soul He has filled with what is good" (Isaiah 58:11, Psalm 107:9).

The craving your soul feels, the spiritual food your soul needs will not be satisfied with fast-food Christianity. Linger slow in God's presence and allow His Word to richly dwell within you, and your soul will be filled, strengthened, and refreshed.

His Present

Oh friends, for soul-filling, "Let the word of Christ richly dwell within you, with all wisdom teaching and admonishing one another with psalms and hymns and spiritual songs, singing with thankfulness in your hearts to God." ~ Colossians 3:16 (NASB)

"Like newborn babies you should crave (thirst for, earnestly desire) the pure (unadulterated) spiritual milk, that by it you may be nurtured and grow unto [completed] salvation." ~ 1 Peter 2:2 (AMPC)

Drink deep, drink long and your soul will be enriched, encouraged, comforted, and overflowing with God's goodness.

Flooding Fear

News reports of attacks, death, battles, wars, and the absolute horror of the evil of man against man seems devastating and the mind wants to just shut down. There seems to be no end to the tragedies of life. Bar the windows, lock the doors, keep out anyone and everyone, and run to the shelters.

I understand, I slept with a loaded gun under my pillow for over a year. I've known fear -- deep, dark dreadful fear. The overwhelming presence of evil, the phone call that says you are being watched, the diagnosis that says hope is gone, the hospital room with cries of agony. And it's all just too much. Fear comes like a flood, wave over wave churning up emotions reeling the mind with despair and dread.

I wonder how did the early church go through the terrors they endured? How does the underground church of today make it through their days? How do we boldly move forward? How do we make it through this flooding fear?

Run to The Word!

The other day I watched a video of a situation in Europe that filled me with fear.

I could barely process or think. I couldn't get the images out of my mind, until I opened my Bible and started reading the Psalms. I started in Psalm 1 and kept reading of our awesome God -- His promises, His rescues, His restoration, His unfailing love and peace returned.

God's word is truth which brings peace. The Bible is living water that refreshes the weary soul. Jesus (The Word) said, "These things I have spoken to you, so that in Me you may have peace. In the world you have tribulation but take courage; I have overcome the world." ~ John 16:33 (NASB

Another thing I've found helpful is remembering God will help others through their situation. I am not the Savior. I am to join God in the ways He prompts me – through prayer, financial aid when called for, and perhaps hands-on help. I must remember God's grace is available for every person in need. His grace, His saving grace, His supplying grace, and His grace to walk through difficulties will be there for the person in need.

God doesn't need to give me grace to walk through something I'm not walking through. However, when His Spirit prompts me to do something, I need to do that thing!

One important factor is remembering not to carry the offenses of someone else. It's SO easy to be offended at what is happening in this world and evil is offensive. But don't be offended at God. We can't see the big picture; we don't see how God is working. We must remember God is always in control, and nothing catches Him by surprise. God is loving and He is always good.

God's rescues come in various forms – sometimes through blocking an attack, sometimes through healing, sometimes through various methods that we prefer, but His rescues also come by bringing someone safely into His presence. Satan is behind all the evil, so be offended at him!

If fear is flooding your soul, take your soul to The Savior. Run to God's Word. When you need shelter, run to the shelter of God. When fear is flooding, ride the wave on the shoulders of The One who calms the waves.

His Present

If you would be willing, read the verses below and allow God's truth to wash over you to bring you peace. If possible read the verses aloud. Speak truth into fear and fear will leave.

"So do not fear, for I am with you; do not be dismayed, for I am your God. I will strengthen you and help you; I will uphold you with my righteous right hand." ~ Isaiah 41:10 (NIV)

"For I am the Lord your God, who upholds your right hand, who says to you, 'Do not fear, I will help you.'" ~ Isaiah 41:13 N (NASB)

"If the Lord had not been on our side when people attacked us, they would have swallowed us alive when their anger flared against us; the flood would have engulfed us, the torrent would have swept over us, the raging waters would have swept us away. Praise be to the Lord, who has not let us be torn by their teeth. We have escaped like a bird from the fowler's snare; the snare has been broken, and we have escaped. Our help is in the name of the Lord, the Maker of heaven and earth." ~ Psalm 124:2-8 (NIV)

"Then they cried out to the Lord in their trouble, and he brought them out of their distress. He stilled the storm to a whisper; the waves of the sea were hushed. They were glad when it grew calm, and he guided them to their desired haven." ~ Psalm 107:28-30 (NIV)

"O Lord God of hosts, who is mighty like You, O Lord? Your faithfulness also surrounds You. You rule the raging of the sea; when its waves rise, You still them." ~ Psalm 89:8-9 (NKJV)

"You answer us with awesome and righteous deeds, God our Savior, the hope of all the ends of the earth and of the farthest seas, who formed the mountains by your power, having armed yourself with strength, who stilled the roaring of the seas, the roaring of their waves, and the turmoil of the nations. The whole earth is filled with awe at your wonders; where morning dawns, where evening fades, you call forth songs of joy." ~ Psalm 65:5-8 (NIV)

Cut the chains

Out of left field a thought came and blindsided my emotions. Words said by someone in the past replayed in my mind entangling me in a web of anger and hurt.

Fortunately, I realized I have a choice. I could think about, whine about, and get mad about what they did, or I could cut the chains that tangle my emotions. Jesus has given a key to freedom, and forgiveness is the ax that cuts us free. As I forgave that person, I could feel the chains that tied me to that person, and the negative thoughts and emotions, lose their hold and I floated free. The weight released and I felt light as a feather. The person remained chained to their sin, but I was free.

Jesus tells us, "If you forgive those who sin against you, your heavenly Father will forgive you. But if you refuse to forgive others, your Father will not forgive your sins" (Matthew 6:14-15) When we forgive, forgiveness leads to our freedom and our forgiveness. Satan wants us to think forgiveness lets the other person off the hook, but the only one unhooked is the one who forgives.

When you forgive, the chain that binds you to that person is cut. Jesus Christ gives forgiveness and freedom so you can cut the chain through forgiveness so you can fly free.

Feeling chained? Cut the chain by forgiving so you can fly free.

His Present

"To be a Christian means to forgive the inexcusable, because God has forgiven the inexcusable in you."
~ C. S. Lewis

"It is not on our forgiveness any more than on our goodness that the world's healing hinges, but His. When He tells us to love our enemies, He gives, along with the command, the love itself."
~ Corrie Ten Boom

For your freedom, to free yourself, cut the chains by forgiving so that you can fly free. "For if you forgive people their trespasses [their reckless and willful sins, leaving them, letting them go, and giving up resentment], your heavenly Father will also forgive you. But if you do not forgive others their trespasses [their reckless and willful sins, leaving them, letting them go, and giving up resentment], neither will your Father forgive you your trespasses."   "It was for freedom that Christ set us free." ~ Matthew 6:14-15 (AMPC), Galatians 5:1 (NIV).

My time

After a long day, I breathed a sigh of relief. Wrapped tight in my blankets, my head nestled in my pillow, I settled in for what I hoped would be a good night's sleep.

Then, when all was quiet, thoughts and worries attacked about the past, present, future, friends, family, the world, politics, and a million other thoughts zinged around in my head. Ack!

I tossed and turned and felt so very helpless, until I remembered sleep is a gift from God. Paul reminds us as Christians we have the power to take our thoughts captive. Therefore, I can tell those troublesome thoughts they have no right to infringe on my time, the time given to me by God for rest, and they can just wait until morning.

I mentally held up my hand and wagged my finger at those annoying thoughts and told them, "No! God gave me this time, and this is my time to sleep. Go away!" Y'all it worked! My thoughts settled, and I drifted off to sleep.

Even if concerns are real and worrisome, we can fight back with God's truth and God's word.

We don't need to be anxious about anything, we can cast our cares on the Lord, trust Him, rely on Him and bring everything to Him, which means we can rest in God's care. We can truly rest.

When those anxious thoughts come a calling, call on Jesus. Your time, daytime or nighttime, you can rest in God's care. "Come to Me, ...and I will give you rest." ~ Matthew 11:28

His Present

God has given you time, time to rest in His presence, time to nourish your soul. When thoughts and worries attack, attack back with God's truth.

The following verses are life and truth to guard your heart and mind.

"Rest in the Lord. Take every thought captive to make it obey Christ, casting all your anxiety on Him, because He cares for you. Be anxious for nothing, but in everything by prayer and supplication with thanksgiving let your requests be made known to God. And the peace of God, which surpasses all comprehension, will guard your hearts and your minds in Christ Jesus.

When you lie down, you will not be afraid; when you lie down, your sleep will be sweet." ~ Psalm 37:7, 2 Corinthians 10:5, 1 Peter 5:7, Philippians 4:6-7, Proverbs 3:24

"Return to your rest, O my soul. The Lord is my light and my salvation; whom shall I fear? The Lord is the defense of my life; whom shall I dread? Those who know Your name will put their trust in You, for You, O Lord, have not forsaken those who seek You. I will lie down and sleep peacefully, for you, Lord, make me safe and secure." ~ Psalm 116:7, Psalm 27:1, Psalm 9:10, Psalm 4:8

Withheld to be held

God's kindness often graciously withholds things to keep me from holding the wrong things. Far too often, the need for human acceptance, accolades, friendships, being noticed by others, have been hindrances in my life.

The approval of man is fickle and changes moment to moment, and the need for attention from people never satisfies because the flesh has an unending appetite for fleshly desires. Encouragement is needed, but when the desire is on receiving attention from people, the need for encouragement becomes an idol.

I haven't always listened to God, haven't always followed His commands, and I've tried to hold onto things that weren't God's best. The result has never been good.

Jesus said to seek first the kingdom of God and to love the Lord with all your heart, soul, mind and strength. These aren't commands to make us miserable, they are blessings that set us free.

I'm learning as I focus on God, seek Him, love Him above all else, everything falls into place.

God is a good Father. He is loving, just, righteous, and all-knowing. God withholds no good thing from those who love Him. Therefore, if I haven't received something I desire, it's because that desire is not good for me at that moment or for long-term.

As I continue on life's journey, I can see SO many times the Lord kept me safe by not giving me something I thought I wanted. The people, the things I thought I needed, were withheld so that God could bless me with His best.

I thought many things would be different in my life, yet how joyous to look back and see God's hand leading and guiding through the highs and lows. Even the hardest things have been renewed and restored.

Hindsight is 20/20, and a friend shared that hindsight is often God's sight. We can't see the future, but God does, and He knows what is best. We can trust God when something is withheld. God is good, we can trust Him, and we can trust His timing.

As we seek His grace, He lets go of our sins, but He never lets go of us.

No matter what seems to be withheld in your life, trust God. Someday, you will understand and see God's loving hand guiding and leading you for, and to, your best.

His Present

I look back at my life and am SO very thankful that God in His loving-kindness and mercy withheld some of the things (and people) I had requested. In hindsight I can see where God withheld what I thought was good so that He could give His best. And, how grateful I am God does not withhold His mercy.

"It seems it was good for me to go through all those troubles. Throughout them all you held tight to my lifeline. You never let me tumble over the edge into nothing. But my sins you let go of, threw them over your shoulder—good riddance!" ~ Isaiah 38:17 (MSG)

God holds us tight through times of hardship and doesn't withhold anything good. "When I said, my foot is slipping, Your mercy and loving-kindness, O Lord, held me up. If God hadn't been there for me, I never would have made it. The minute I said, 'I'm slipping, I'm falling,' your love, God, took hold and held me fast. For the Lord God is a sun and shield; the Lord gives grace and glory; no good thing does He withhold from those who walk uprightly." ~ Psalm 94:18 (AMPC), Psalm 94:17-18 (MSG), Psalm 84:11 (NASB)

God is with you through every step of your way. "Guide me into your truth and teach me. For you are the God who delivers me; on you I rely all day long. For You are my rock and my fortress; for Your name's sake You will lead me and guide me. If I ascend to heaven, You are there; if I make my bed in Sheol, behold, You are there. If I take the wings of the dawn, if I dwell in the remotest part of the sea, even there Your hand will lead me, and Your right hand will lay hold of me." ~ Psalm 25:5 (NET Bible), Psalm 31:3 (NASB), Psalm 139:8-10 (NASB)

"I have held many things in my hands, and I have lost them all; but whatever I have placed in God's hands, that I still possess." ~ Corrie Ten Boom

Never dry

The sun peeked over the horizon and a bird sang outside the window welcoming the dawn. I nestled in the chair for much-needed time with God. My soul was tired and parched, and I was desperate to hear from God. God's word beckoned, "Arise, shine; for your light has come, and the glory of the Lord has risen upon you (Isaiah 60:1 NASB)

I needed God's light, I needed His glory to shine on my weary soul. I had stepped off social media, stepped away to sort through how I was supposed to find a balance in writing, interacting with people online and in my personal life. Like Jeremiah, God's word burns in my bones, and I must share, but I couldn't find the balance.

I want to be like Paul, like others who have gone before running their race, carrying the torch of Christ in the relay of the Christian life. I want to be like the athlete who left all on the playing field, tired because they've given their all, but with a good, happy-tired, as they played their hardest and their best.

As I sequestered myself, I expected a monk-like pursuit of God, long and tedious while God wrestled out anything that kept me hindered and upset. However, God pleasantly surprised me. As I sat, allowing my soul to still in God's presence, His truths came rushing and gushing into my parched soul.

God's truth reminded me that God's well doesn't run dry. The well of Christ NEVER runs dry.

Jesus is the Living Water always living and bringing soul-hydration. Time is limited, I don't need to limit myself, or my time, by thinking I don't have what I need. I need to stop thinking, worrying, leaning on my own understanding, instead I must keep my focus on Jesus, in all my ways acknowledge Him and He will direct my steps. By reading and then meditating on God's word, I can be like a long-distance runner wearing a water bottle on their back, continuing to run while drawing deep from The Living Water.

Yes, there are times to retreat from the world. Jesus often went to be alone with His Father, yet He stayed the course, kept His eye on the prize, and finished the Father's will. As ambassadors for Christ, we are chosen before the foundation of the world to proclaim His excellencies, bringing glory to God. By staying in God's word, *The Word*, our souls will never run dry. We can continue sharing, living, rejoicing in the constant hydration of the living water.

We are more than conquerors in Christ. Therefore, we can live in the vibrancy of our living Christ. God supplies and equips. In Christ, no necessary need will go unmet.

Join me and let's live deep in the deep things of God. Keep reading God's word and The Living Water will keep you filled. Keep going. Run with endurance, keep your eyes on the prize and continue sharing about our wonderful God. Sing, speak, write, and proclaim the glories of our glorious Savior.

Enjoy the journey God has given. Sing His praises, shout for joy, keep running fully immersed in the living water and you will never run dry.

His Present

As you read the following verses, take note of all the ways God's Word brings life, direction, and refreshing.

"The law of the Lord is perfect, refreshing the soul. The statutes of the Lord are trustworthy, making wise the simple. The precepts of the Lord are right, giving joy to the heart. The commands of the Lord are radiant, giving light to the eyes. The fear of the Lord is pure, enduring forever. The decrees of the Lord are firm, and all of them are righteous. They are more precious than gold, than much pure gold; they are sweeter than honey, than honey from the honeycomb." ~ Psalm 19:7-10 (NIV)

"Oh, the joys of those who do not follow the advice of the wicked, or stand around with sinners, or join in with mockers. But they delight in the law of the Lord, meditating on it day and night. They are like trees planted along the riverbank, bearing fruit each season. Their leaves never wither, and they prosper in all they do." ~ Psalm 1:1-3 (NLT)

"This book of the law shall not depart from your mouth, but you shall meditate on it day and night, so that you may be careful to do according to all that is written in it; for then you will make your way prosperous, and then you will have success." ~ Joshua 1:8 (NASB)

"He who believes in Me [who cleaves to and trusts in and relies on Me] as the Scripture has said, from his innermost being shall flow [continuously] springs and rivers of living water." ~ John 7:38 (AMPC)

"Do you not know that in a race all the runners compete, but [only] one receives the prize? So run [your race] that you may lay hold [of the prize] and make it yours." ~ 1 Corinthians 9:24 (AMPC)

Not

In Christ, you are ...

Not lost.
For the Son of Man has come to seek and to save that which was lost. And I give them eternal life, and they shall never perish; neither shall anyone snatch them out of My hand. My Father, who has given them to Me, is greater than all; and no one is able to snatch them out of My Father's hand (Luke 19:10 NASB, John 10:28-29 NKJV).

Not forsaken.
Those who know Your name will put their trust in You, for You, O Lord, have not forsaken those who seek You. For the Lord loves justice and does not forsake His godly ones; they are preserved forever. For the Lord will not cast off His people, nor will He forsake His inheritance. (Psalm 9:10 NASB, Psalm 37:28 NASB, Psalm 94:14 NKJV).

Not forgotten.
Can a woman forget her nursing child and have no compassion on the son of her womb? Even these may forget, but I will not forget you (Isaiah 49:15 NASB).

Not alone.
And the Lord, He is the One who goes before you. He will be with you, He will not leave you nor

forsake you; do not fear nor be dismayed. I am with you always, even to the end of the age. (Deuteronomy 31:8, Matthew 28:20 NKJV)

Not abandoned.

I was once young, now I am old. I have never seen a godly man abandoned, or his children forced to search for food. Even if my father and mother abandoned me, the Lord would take me in (Psalm 37:25 NET Bible, Psalm 27:10 NET Bible).

Not shaken.

So let us be thankful because we have a kingdom that cannot be shaken.... (Hebrews 12:28 NCV).

Not without hope.

Blessed be the God and Father of our Lord Jesus Christ, who according to His great mercy has caused us to be born again to a living hope through the resurrection of Jesus Christ from the dead (1 Peter 1:3 NASB).

Not without family and not without a Father.

A father of the fatherless, a defender of widows, is God in His holy habitation Because you are sons, God has sent forth the Spirit of His Son into our hearts, crying, "Abba! Father!". For whoever does the will of My Father who is in heaven, he is My brother and sister and mother. "And I will be a father to you, and you shall be sons and daughters to Me," Says the Lord Almighty (Psalm 68:5 NKJV,

Galatians 4:6 NASB, Matthew 12:50 NASB, 2 Corinthians 6:18 NASB).

His Present

Heavenly Father, thank You that You loved me so much that Jesus came so I would not perish but have eternal life. Thank You that You have not turned away my prayer or Your mercy. I will not be afraid. You enlarge the path under me so my feet will not slip. You are my rock, my salvation, my defense, I shall not be moved. Therefore, I will bless You Lord and forget not all of Your benefits.

Thank You that I am not lost, not forsaken, not forgotten, not alone, not abandoned, not shaken, not without hope, not without family, and not without a Father. Thank You!

Scripture Reference: John 3:14-17 (NKJV), Psalm 66:20 (NKJV), Psalm 56:11 (NKJV), Psalm 18:36 (NKJV), Psalm 62:6 (NKJV), Psalm 103:2 (NKJV)

The old

I've heard people say they don't like the Old Testament and therefore they didn't read or study anything in the Bible earlier than the New Testament. Please don't ignore the Old Testament. Throughout God's Word, we read of His consistent, constant love and affection for His people, and His desire for relationship with His children.

The Old Testament reveals God's justice, righteousness, protection, and commandments given to keep His people to keep them safe and help them live godly lives for peace and prosperity.

The Old Testament tells the stories of those who have gone before us, those who failed and yet were restored by God. The Old Testament tells of God's tender mercies to people even though they wandered from Him, ignored Him, and turned their backs on Him.

The Old Testament blesses us with the stories of Moses, Noah, David, Esther, Ruth and Boaz, and so many others who reveal God uses the ordinary for extraordinary assignments. The Old Testament gave us the Psalms. The Old Testament shows God's unfailing love. The Old Testament is a stepping stone to lead to the new covenant of God's redemption for a fallen world. The Old Testament points to Jesus Christ.

God said, His people were destroyed for lack of knowledge (Hosea 4:6) because the priests of that time were not teaching correctly, they were twisting and manipulating God's teachings for their own gain.

For our protection, we need to know God's word for ourselves. We need to be aware of the truth in every part of God's word.

God's Word brings knowledge and protection against the enemy and those who twist and manipulate for their own gain and ambition.

Paul reminds us every Scripture is God-breathed for instruction, reproof, conviction of sin, correction of error, discipline in obedience, training in righteousness, so that we are thoroughly equipped for every good work. If we aren't reading God's word – all of God's word – then we will not be thoroughly equipped.

Treasure awaits in the Word of God. Jesus said, "every teacher and interpreter of the Sacred Writings who has been instructed about and trained for the kingdom of heaven and has become a disciple is like a householder who brings forth out of his storehouse treasure that is new and [treasure that is] old [the fresh as well as the familiar]." ~ Matthew 13:52 (AMPC)

When Jesus rebuked Satan, Jesus quoted scripture from what we know as the Old Testament. God's word gives us power to fight against the enemy. God's Word is our sword of truth.

Please make the time to study the Bible for yourself, for your protection, knowledge, and to find the treasure and joy that awaits those who search.

His Present

Remember to, "Study and be eager and do your utmost to present yourself to God approved (tested by trial), a workman who has no cause to be ashamed, correctly analyzing and accurately dividing [rightly handling and skillfully teaching] the Word of Truth." ~ 2 Timothy 2:15 (AMPC)

"Every Scripture is God-breathed (given by His inspiration) and profitable for instruction, for reproof and conviction of sin, for correction of error and discipline in obedience, [and] for training in righteousness (in holy living, in conformity to God's will in thought, purpose, and action), so that the man of God may be complete and proficient, well fitted and thoroughly equipped for every good work." ~ 2 Timothy 3:16-17 (AMPC)

"For you have been born again, but not to a life that will quickly end. Your new life will last forever because it comes from the eternal, living word of God." "For the Word that God speaks is alive and full of power [making it active, operative, energizing, and effective]; it is sharper than any two-edged sword, penetrating to the dividing line of the breath of life (soul) and [the immortal] spirit, and of joints and marrow [of the deepest parts of our nature], exposing and sifting and analyzing and judging the very thoughts and purposes of the heart." ~ 1 Peter 1:23 (NLT), Hebrews 4:12 (AMPC)

"Stand firm therefore, by fastening the belt of truth around your waist, by putting on the breastplate of righteousness, by fitting your feet with the preparation that comes from the good news of peace, and in all of this, by taking up the shield of faith with which you can extinguish all the flaming arrows of the evil one. And take the helmet of salvation and the sword of the Spirit, which is the word of God." ~ Ephesians 6:14-17 (NET Bible)

And finally, "Let the word of Christ dwell in you richly in all wisdom, teaching and admonishing one another in psalms and hymns and spiritual songs, singing with grace in your hearts to the Lord." ~ Colossians 3:16 (NKJV)

Celebrating holidays

Loved ones are no longer with us, the days are shorter, darker, and colder. The season says celebrate, but it's hard sometimes, difficult to even think about decorating and celebrating. Last year I didn't get out our big Christmas tree, instead I bought a tiny one to sit on a table in the family room representing only a snippet of the holidays.

As I pondered the season, I remembered it's not about who is not with us, or what we have or don't have, it's about Who is with us Immanuel – God with us -- and what He has given us --- eternal life, unfailing love, peace, hope, and joy.

Therefore, I've decorated inside and outside the house. I decorated and hummed Christmas songs as I celebrated the true meaning of Christmas, the true reason to celebrate the holidays. Christ is with us which means our joy, our reason to celebrate, is always with us.

No matter how alone we may be, or how we may feel, regardless of current circumstances, we are never alone with Christ living in our hearts. We've been given eternal life in Christ; the joy of heaven came from heaven to bless us with His joy.

In Christ, we have peace that remains for we live in an eternal kingdom. In Christ, we are given a living hope that never leaves us hopeless.

Celebrate the truth, the reality, of a God who loved you so very much, that He sent His Son to rescue you. Jesus willingly laid down His life, to die for your sins, He rose again, and opened His nail-scarred hands to welcome you into His forever family. Celebrate the beauty of unfailing love.

Regardless of the calendar, no matter what life holds, you are always held securely in the love of Christ. Will you join me in celebrating?

His Present

Christmas is the gift of God through His Son, Jesus Christ, "The angel said to them, 'Do not be afraid; for behold, I bring you good news of great joy which will be for all the people; for today in the city of David there has been born for you a Savior, who is Christ the Lord. ...And suddenly there appeared with the angel a multitude of the heavenly host praising God and saying, 'Glory to God in the highest, and on earth peace among men with whom He is pleased.'" ~ Luke 2:10-14 (NASB)

Rejoice in the new life you have been given. "All praise to God, the Father of our Lord Jesus Christ. It is by his great mercy that we have been born again, because God raised Jesus Christ from the dead. Now we live with great expectation." ~ 1 Peter 1:3 (NLT)

Because we have been given Jesus, because we have the hope of eternal life, rejoice today, rejoice tomorrow, rejoice forever. "Always be full of joy in the Lord. I say it again—rejoice! Let everyone see that you are considerate in all you do. Remember, the Lord is coming soon. Don't worry about anything; instead, pray about everything. Tell God what you need and thank him for all he has done.

Then you will experience God's peace, which exceeds anything we can understand. His peace will guard your hearts and minds as you live in Christ Jesus." ~ Philippians 4:4-7 (NLT)

Loving All

I've been struggling with feelings of inadequacy in a few areas. Then I realized ALL the many promises God has given those who put their faith and trust in His Son, Jesus Christ. I've listed just a fraction of ALL the beautiful promises God has given in His word.

As I made this list, I could feel my inadequate feelings fade away and my confidence grow. God is a loving Father and His promises are to us, for us for all the days of our lives.

Read slow and linger in the beauty of His love.

"Your eyes have seen my unformed substance; and in Your book were **all** written the days that were ordained for me, when as yet there was not one of them." ~ Psalm 139:16 (NASB)

"My God will supply **all** your needs according to His riches in glory in Christ Jesus." ~ Philippians 4:19 (NASB)

"Be anxious for nothing, but in everything by prayer and supplication with thanksgiving let your requests be made known to God. And the peace of God, which surpasses **all** comprehension, will guard your hearts and your minds in Christ Jesus." ~ Philippians 4:6-7 (NASB)

"Give **all** your worries to Him because He cares for you." ~ 1 Peter 5:7 (NLV)

"In **all** your ways acknowledge Him, and He will make your paths straight." ~ Proverbs 3:6 (NASB)

"The Lord keeps **all** who love Him, but **all** the wicked He will destroy." ~ Psalm 145:20 (NASB)

"For He will give His angels charge concerning you, to guard you in **all** your ways." ~ Psalm 91:11 (NASB)

"Surely goodness and lovingkindness will follow me **all** the days of my life, and I will dwell in the house of the Lord forever." ~ Psalm 23:6 (NASB)

"Let the word of Christ richly dwell within you, with **all** wisdom teaching and admonishing one another with psalms and hymns and spiritual songs, singing with thankfulness in your hearts to God." ~ Colossians 3:16 (NASB)

"For as many as are the promises of God, they **all** find their Yes [answer] in Him [Christ]. For this reason we also utter the Amen (so be it) to God through Him [in His Person and by His agency] to the glory of God." ~ 2 Corinthians 1:20 (AMPC)

"Now to Him who is able to do far more abundantly beyond **all** that we ask or think, according to the power that works within us, to Him be the glory in the church and in Christ Jesus to all generations forever and ever. Amen." ~ Ephesians 3:20-21 (NASB)

No matter what comes your way, what time you have on this earth, and what task you are given, God will supply **ALL** your needs, All the days of your life. Fully live this life God has given, living and loving all His blessings, all His promises, and love Him always with ALL that is within you.

His Present

Jesus said, "You shall love the Lord your God with **all** your heart, and with **all** your soul, and with **all** your mind.' ~ Matthew 22:37 (NASB)

As we love God with all that is within us, God's love can pour deeper within us.

Ponder all the ways you are loved by God, and all the ways you can love God. God loves you all the days you have on earth and all the days you will be in heaven. You are loved!

"Bless the Lord, O my soul, and **all** that is within me, bless His holy name." ~ Psalm 103:1 (NASB)

Recalculating

I plugged our route into our GPS for the trip back home. Returning from visiting my parents, sweet hubby and I decided to take different roads to avoid the Natchez Trace Parkway. Although the parkway had been beautiful on our trip down to see my folks, the isolated road at night didn't seem like the best idea.

As we neared the turnoff, the GPS advised us to take the parkway. We ignored the suggestion, passed the intersection, and the GPS directed us to turn around. Even as we traveled several more miles, it continued to summon us to return to the parkway. Finally, after several more miles, the GPS finally recalculated the route. Fortunately, it didn't shame us, yell at us, or say we had made a big mistake, it rerouted based on our progress and continued to guide us forward.

I often route my day based on what I think I need to accomplish. But then life happens, and plans get changed. I can yell, whine, and complain, or keep moving forward and see what God has planned. What I often see as interruptions are divine appointments.

Expectations are sometimes in contradiction to how God works and moves. I like to plan my day, my life... but Jesus says "Follow Me." Following Jesus is not a straight line, He leads through mountains and valleys, through the wild and crazy, good and bad, and through the boring and mundane. He promises to lead us, to be with us through each and every step. I'm trying to learn that the journey isn't only about a destination, it's about following and living in the moment in the presence of The One who longs to be present in our lives.

The only calculating needed to make on our journey, is to make sure we're following Jesus. We can rest assured; His direction and guidance will never take us the wrong way.

His Present

As you read God's word, remember you are given direction, guidance, and the joy of His presence.

"Your word is a lamp to my feet and a light to my path." ~ Psalm 119:105 (NASB)

"Make me know Your ways, O Lord; teach me Your paths." ~ Psalm 25:4 (NASB)

"With Your counsel You will guide me, and afterward receive me to glory." ~ Psalm 73:24 (NASB)

"For You are my rock and my fortress; for Your name's sake You will lead me and guide me." ~ Psalm 31:3 (NASB)

"You will make known to me the path of life; in Your presence is fullness of joy; in Your right hand there are pleasures forever." ~ Psalm 16:11 (NASB)

"When you walk about, they will guide you; when you sleep, they will watch over you; and when you awake, they will talk to you." ~ Proverbs 6:22 (NASB)

"Your ears will hear a word behind you, 'This is the way, walk in it,' whenever you turn to the right or to the left." ~ Isaiah 30:21 (NASB)

"He restores my soul; He guides me in the paths of righteousness for His name's sake." ~ Psalm 23:3 (NASB)

"All the paths of the Lord are lovingkindness and truth to those who keep His covenant and His testimonies! ~ Psalm 25:10 (NASB)

Come to the Manger

Soft and quiet, nine months in the womb, infinite born to bring infinite grace to the finite. Joy split the sky open as angels sang of amazing grace-filled glory. God's love moved to allow man to move into God's love. The Good News from heaven bringing good news to all mankind.

A babe in swaddling clothes, divine in humanity to grant humanity access to the divine. The cry of The Word became flesh. Tiny hands that once held the universe, earth-bound to dwell among men. His birth birthing eternal life. Hope in humanity bringing hope to all humanity. Jesus, Immanuel, God with us, to bring God to us.

The manger built by a carpenter to hold the carpenter's son, cradles the cradle of life. A feeding trough for those who are hungry holds the bread of life for hungry souls. The manger, an ark to carry The One who will carry us through the rough waters of life.

The shepherds hurried to the manger to see The One spoken of by the angels.

The Wise Men traveled far to worship and bring gifts to the long-awaited Messiah.

No matter how long you've waited, come.

No matter how long it's taken, come.

Come to the manger. Come to the Messiah.

Bring yourself, your gifts, and your worship. Whatever you've been through, whatever you face, whatever your heartache and pain, bring to the manger. For the manger is new life, hope, joy, and new beginnings.

Whatever is in your heart, bring to The One who made your heart. Lay down every burden, for

God's love waits in the manger.

Will you come?

The Messiah, the Savior in the manger, moves into your heart so you are never alone, never forsaken, never without hope, never without joy, never without peace, never without life eternal.

Please come...

His Present

Mary "gave birth to her firstborn son; and she wrapped Him in cloths, and laid Him in a manger, because there was no room for them in the inn. In the same region there were some shepherds staying out in the fields and keeping watch over their flock by night. And an angel of the Lord suddenly stood before them, and the glory of the Lord shone around them; and they were terribly frightened. But the angel said to them, 'Do not be afraid; for behold, I bring you good news of great joy which will be for all the people; for today in the city of David there has been born for you a Savior, who is Christ the Lord. This will be a sign for you: you will find a baby wrapped in cloths and lying in a manger.' And suddenly there appeared with the angel a multitude of the heavenly host praising God and saying, 'Glory to God in the highest, and on earth peace among men with whom He is pleased.' When the angels had gone away from them into heaven, the shepherds began saying to one another, 'Let us go straight to Bethlehem then, and see this thing that has happened which the Lord has made known to us.' So they came in a hurry and found their way to Mary and Joseph, and the baby as He lay in the manger." ~ Luke 2:7-16 (NASB)

"For God so loved the world, that He gave His only begotten Son, that whoever believes in Him shall not perish, but have eternal life." ~ John 3:16 (NASB)

Will you come?

Dance of the frail

As disease continues to ravage my friend's body, the outside world thinks she has no life, no connections, and no hope. Oh, but my bedridden friend, frail as she may be, dances with Jesus. She communes with her Savior. Her body is trapped, but her spirit continues to soar and be free. Her prayers rise to the heavens unhindered by time or space.

Our bodies, our frailties, our lack of certain skills, may hinder us in the earthly, but in the heavenlies things are different.

The dance of the frail, the song of the tone deaf, are all beautiful to our Heavenly Father.

Bedridden, clumsy, elderly, body difficulties, do no matter in a dance on The Father's grace-filled toes. Lack of skill doesn't matter when in the carpentry shop with The Father. Weakness or inadequacies do not ever disqualify our Father's love.

Life in Christ is life in abundance, life with guidance, life in accordance to God's loving will. Oh, the abundant life given through Christ gives us His power, His strength, His wisdom, His love, to soul-dance forever with Him.

Dance in the grace of Jesus, dance in the love of The Father, dance forever with our forever God.

His Present

"The Lord says, 'I will guide you along the best pathway for your life. I will advise you and watch over you.'" ~ Psalm 32:8 (NLT)

"Don't be afraid, for I am with you. Don't be discouraged, for I am your God. I will strengthen you and help you. I will hold you up with my victorious right hand." ~ Isaiah 41:10 (NLT)

"For I hold you by your right hand— I, the Lord your God. And I say to you, 'Don't be afraid. I am here to help you.'" ~ Isaiah 41:13 (NLT)

"I will be your God throughout your lifetime— until your hair is white with age. I made you, and I will care for you. I will carry you along and save you." ~ Isaiah 46:4 (NLT)

Thank you

I'm honored, very honored, you took the time to read this devotional. Thank you.

My hope is that the book provided encouragement and helped you on your journey.

Keep seeking God, drawing near to Him, loving Him, and rest in the presence of your loving, almighty Heavenly Father.

"Now may our Lord Jesus Christ Himself, and our God and Father, who has loved us and given us everlasting consolation and good hope by grace, comfort your hearts and establish you in every good word and work." ~ 2 Thessalonians 2:16-17 (NKJV)

About the Author

Lisa Buffaloe is a happily married mom, author, and speaker. When she's not writing, she enjoys working in her yard, exploring God's beautiful nature, and taking long walks with her sweet husband.

Lisa loves sharing God's unending love and that through Him we find healing, restoration, renewal, and joy.

Visit Lisa at https://lisabuffaloe.com.

Books by Lisa Buffaloe

(Updated July 2023)

Fiction

The Masterpiece Beneath
Nadia's Hope (Hope and Grace Series, Book 1)
  Prodigal Nights (Hope and Grace Series, 2)
  Writing Her Heart (Hope and Grace Series, 3)
  The Discovery Chapter (Hope and Grace Series, 4)
  Open Lens (Hope and Grace Series, 5)
The Fortune
Grace for the Char-Baked

Non-Fiction

Float by Faith
Heart and Soul Medication
Time with The Timeless One
The Forgotten Resting Place
Present in His Presence
We Were Meant for Paradise
One Lit Step: Devotions for your journey
The Unnamed Devotional
Flying on His Wings
Unfailing Treasures
No Wound Too Deep for The Deep Love of Christ
Living Joyfully Free Devotional, (Volume 1)
Living Joyfully Free Devotional, (Volume 2)

Bible credits

Because the original text of the Bible was written in Hebrew, Aramaic, and Greek, the original language is rich and full. The various Bible versions I use during writing are to find the one most appropriate showing the beauty and the truth of each scripture.

Scripture taken from the New Century Version® (NCV). Copyright © 2005 by Thomas Nelson, Inc. Used by permission. All rights reserved.

Living Bible (TLB) The Living Bible copyright © 1971 by Tyndale House Foundation. Used by permission of Tyndale House Publishers Inc., Carol Stream, Illinois 60188. All rights reserved.

Scripture quotations taken from the New American Standard Bible®(NASB), Copyright © 1960, 1962, 1963, 1968, 1971, 1972, 1973, 1975, 1977, 1995 by The Lockman Foundation Used by permission. www.Lockman.org"

Scripture quotations marked (NLT) are taken from the Holy Bible, New Living Translation, copyright © 1996, 2004, 2007 by Tyndale House Foundation. Used by permission of Tyndale House Publishers, Inc., Carol Stream, Illinois 60188. All rights reserved.

THE HOLY BIBLE, NEW INTERNATIONAL VERSION®, NIV® Copyright © 1973, 1978, 1984, 2011 by Biblica, Inc.™ Used by permission. All rights reserved worldwide.

NET Bible® copyright ©1996-2006 by Biblical Studies Press, L.L.C. http://netbible.com

Scripture taken from the New King James Version®. Copyright © 1982 by Thomas Nelson, Inc. Used by permission. All rights reserved.

The ESV® Bible (The Holy Bible, English Standard Version®). ESV® Text Edition: 2016. Copyright © 2001 by Crossway, a publishing ministry of Good News Publishers. The ESV® text has been reproduced in cooperation with and by permission of Good News Publishers. Unauthorized reproduction of this publication is prohibited. All rights reserved.

Scripture taken from *The Message*. Copyright © 1993, 1994, 1995, 1996, 2000, 2001, 2002. Used by permission of NavPress Publishing Group.

Scripture quotations taken from the New Life Version (NLV) Copyright © 1969–2003 by Christian Literature International, P.O. Box 777, Canby, OR 97013. Used by permission.

Scripture quotations taken from the Amplified® Bible (AMP), Copyright © 2015 by The Lockman Foundation Used by permission. www.Lockman.org

Scripture quotations taken from the Amplified® Bible (AMPC), Copyright © 1954, 1958, 1962, 1964, 1965, 1987 by The Lockman Foundation Used by permission. www.Lockman.org

Holman Christian Standard Bible (HCSB) Copyright © 1999, 2000, 2002, 2003, 2009 by Holman Bible Publishers, Nashville Tennessee. All rights reserved.

Thank you for reading,

Present in His Presence

"Now to Him who is able to keep you from stumbling, and to present you faultless before the presence of His glory with exceeding joy, To God our Savior, Who alone is wise, be glory and majesty, dominion and power, both now and forever."
~ Jude 24-25 (NKJV)

www.ingramcontent.com/pod-product-compliance
Lightning Source LLC
Chambersburg PA
CBHW061328040426
42444CB00011B/2817